PRAISE FOR

If I Have to Tell You One More Time . . .

"Just when you thought you had no need for another parenting book, along comes Amy McCready's invaluable guide to raising responsible, caring, well-behaved children. When it comes to helping parents with the day-to-day challenges of raising children—from managing meltdowns to getting kids to do their chores—few books can compete with this one in terms of practical, clear, and wonderfully wise advice."
> —Annie Pleshette Murphy, ABC-TV parenting contributor and author of *The 7 Stages of Motherhood*

"If you've ever found yourself screaming at your kids, wondering, 'How did I lose control?', this is the book for you. Amy McCready shows you how to be the boss without being a bitch."
> —Lisa Earle McLeod, author of *The Triangle of Truth*, a *Washington Post* Top 5 Business Book

"I've always said that if parents do their job right, they eventually work themselves out of a job. Finally: the tools we all need to achieve 'parental unemployment.' And best of all, you never have to get mad."
> —Wendy L. Walsh, Ph.D., human behavior expert on CNN's *Headline News* and mother of two

"I love it: Amy McCready takes the frustration out of trying to get kids to do those boring but necessary tasks. She shows parents how to calmly and confidently—without nagging, berating, or punishing—inspire kids to make positive choices. Packed with clear direction—including really practical tips and simple strategies—for how to put an end to whining, tantrums, battles, and all the rest, this book will be a giant relief for parents who want to bring out the best in their kids."
> —Christine Carter, Ph.D., author of *Raising Happiness: 10 Simple Steps for More Joyful Kids and Happier Parents*

"Amy McCready's *If I Have to Tell You One More Time* is a welcome guide for parents wanting to specifically address problem behaviors. Spoken like a real mom, this revolutionary program will help any parent address any problem . . . with calm."
> —Hal E. Runkel, M.S., MMFT, LMFT, bestselling author of *ScreamFree Parenting* and coauthor of *ScreamFree Marriage*

"This is a brilliant book! Amy McCready understands what's really motivating our children, and gives us a set of simple but effective tools we can use to satisfy their true needs, and bring about an end to all the power struggles and acting out. Practical and wise, this is advice that will change your life—and the lives of your children—forever."

—Dr. Heidi Grant Halvorson, motivational psychologist and researcher, and author of *Succeed: How We Can Reach Our Goals*

"A lot of parenting books promise a 'revolutionary program,' but Amy McCready's *If I Have to Tell You One More Time* actually delivers on that promise. To be a parent without nagging, reminding, or yelling seems the impossible dream, but McCready's well-developed approach combines information and intuition in a completely accessible manner. Every parenting scenario imagined is explained with an easy-to-understand solution provided. This book takes the guesswork out of everyday parenting dilemmas that may have derailed your family. Whether you have toddlers or teens, you'll benefit from the book—and so will your kids!"

—Lian Dolan, parenting expert, Oprah.com, and creator of chaoschronicles.com

"This book should be required reading for parents of children of any age. Reasoned and reasonable, the ideas and strategies McCready offers provide a road map to raising resilient children. I will add this volume to the short list of books I recommend to parents and professionals."

—Sam Goldstein, Ph.D., coauthor of *Raising Resilient Children*, and coeditor of the *Encyclopedia of Child Behavior and Development*

"Amy McCready's encouragement and practical steps will work wonders for building, correcting, and strengthening a positive, healthy connection between parents and children. This book is a gift for parents everywhere."

— Marc and Amy Vachon, authors of *Equally Shared Parenting*

"As we all know, children don't come with an instruction booklet, and parenting can be a daily challenge. Amy McCready helps parents feel empowered, by arming them with easy-to-understand and effective parenting techniques. Her 'toolbox solutions' are just what all parents need to solve everything from day-to-day annoyances to long-term conflicts. I believe that we are not raising children, but are raising adults. Parents who utilize these tools will be giving their children a big step toward being successful grown-ups."

—Stacy Kaiser, licensed psychotherapist and author of *How to Be a Grown Up*

"*If I Have to Tell You One More Time* is packed with easy-to-use tools that empower both parents and children. Amy McCready reveals why many trendy parenting strategies fail and may even inadvertently teach exactly the opposite of what we're trying to instill in our children."

—Jamie Woolf, author of *Mom-in-Chief: How Wisdom from the Workplace Can Save Your Family from Chaos*

"Finally, the instruction manual we've all been searching for to raise caring, responsible, empowered kids."

—Mike Robbins, author of *Focus on the Good Stuff*

"If you wonder whether the neighbors can hear you yelling at your kids day after day, it's time to read Amy McCready's *If I Have to Tell You One More Time*. Once you learn how to discipline instead of punish, with Amy's overflowing toolbox of tips, your kids will listen—and you'll get your voice back."

—Jen Singer, founder of MommaSaid.net and author of *You're a Good Mom (and your kids aren't so bad either)*

"Amy McCready is one smart mama! From her advice to use words of encouragement instead of praise, to her suggestion that parents and children take Mind, Body & Soul Time, to her Toolbox Solutions, Amy's wisdom and experience shine through in *If I Have to Tell You One More Time*. This is a must-read for every parent—and every early childhood professional, for that matter!"

—Rae Pica, host of *Body, Mind and Child* (BAM! Radio Network)

"Amy McCready's practical tools help restore parental sanity while creating a higher quality of life for every family member. Recommended!"

—Amy Tiemann, Ph.D., founder of MojoMom.com and author of *Mojo Mom: Nurturing Your Self While Raising a Family*

"*If I Have to Tell You One More Time* is an absolute must-have guide for all parents who want to take their family from good to great. In a sensible and engaging way, Amy McCready debunks outdated parenting myths while equipping parents with practical solutions for successfully handling a variety of child-rearing challenges. Offering a blueprint for getting to the root cause of misbehaviors, McCready also provides a comprehensive array of tools to help parents understand when and why these strategies work, along with superb action-oriented tips."

—Christina McGhee, author of *Parenting Apart: How Separated and Divorced Parents Can Raise Happy and Secure Kids*

"Doesn't the most important job of your life deserve some fabulous training? Take the strife out of family life with this indispensable toolbox for parents who want to empower their children toward their own success. Bravo!"

—Dana Bedford Hilmer, host of *LifestyleMom Radio Café* and editor of *Blindsided by a Diaper*

"So many times after reading parenting books we're left thinking, 'Sounds good. But now what do I do?' Amy McCready's simple, from-the-trenches tools provide a step-by-step process to deflect the negative power struggles you don't want, and give you more of what you do want—cooperation, responsibility, respect, and family fun!"

—Robyn J. A. Silverman, Ph.D., child/teen development expert and author of *Good Girls Don't Get Fat: How Weight Obsession Is Messing Up Our Girls and How We Can Help Them Thrive Despite It*

"Destined to become a classic among parenting books, because it helps you parent from the heart—instead of trying to remember some obscure intellectual formula that vanishes in the heat of the moment. Give your children the connection they're longing for (yes, even teens!) and watch their misbehavior transform before your very eyes. I especially love how McCready emphasizes the need for parents to assess the effectiveness of their own patterns as well. If only I'd had this book from the very beginning!"

—Jennifer Newcomb Marine, coauthor of *No One's the Bitch: A Ten-Step Plan for the Mother and Stepmother Relationship*

If I
HAVE to
TELL *You*
ONE
MORE
TIME...

The Revolutionary Program That Gets Your Kids
to Listen Without Nagging, Reminding, or Yelling

Amy McCready

JEREMY P. TARCHER / PENGUIN
a member of Penguin Group (USA) Inc.
New York

JEREMY P. TARCHER/PENGUIN
Published by the Penguin Group

Penguin Group (USA) Inc., 375 Hudson Street, New York, New York 10014, USA • Penguin Group (Canada), 90 Eglinton Avenue East, Suite 700, Toronto, Ontario M4P 2Y3, Canada (a division of Pearson Penguin Canada Inc.) • Penguin Books Ltd, 80 Strand, London WC2R 0RL, England • Penguin Ireland, 25 St Stephen's Green, Dublin 2, Ireland (a division of Penguin Books Ltd) • Penguin Group (Australia), 250 Camberwell Road, Camberwell, Victoria 3124, Australia (a division of Pearson Australia Group Pty Ltd) • Penguin Books India Pvt Ltd, 11 Community Centre, Panchsheel Park, New Delhi–110 017, India • Penguin Group (NZ), 67 Apollo Drive, Rosedale, North Shore 0632, New Zealand (a division of Pearson New Zealand Ltd) • Penguin Books (South Africa) (Pty) Ltd, 24 Sturdee Avenue, Rosebank, Johannesburg 2196, South Africa

Penguin Books Ltd, Registered Offices: 80 Strand, London WC2R 0RL, England

First trade paperback edition 2012
Copyright © 2011 by Amy McCready

Most Tarcher/Penguin books are available at special quantity discounts for bulk purchase for sales promotions, premiums, fund-raising, and educational needs. Special books or book excerpts also can be created to fit specific needs. For details, write Penguin Group (USA) Inc. Special Markets, 375 Hudson Street, New York, NY 10014.

The Library of Congress catalogued the hardcover edition as follows:

McCready, Amy.
If I have to tell you one more time . . . : the revolutionary program that gets your kids to listen without nagging, reminding or yelling / Amy McCready;
p.   cm.
Includes index.
ISBN 978-1-58542-864-9
1. Child rearing.   2. Child psychology.   3. Parenting.   I. Title.
HQ772.M384   2011   2011007267
649'.64—dc22

ISBN 978-0-399-16059-2 (paperback edition)

Printed in the United States of America
17   19   20   18

BOOK DESIGN BY TANYA MAIBORODA

Neither the publisher nor the author is engaged in rendering professional advice or services to the individual reader. The ideas, procedures, and suggestions contained in this book are not intended as a substitute for consulting with your physician. All matters regarding your health require medical supervision. Neither the author nor the publisher shall be liable or responsible for any loss or damage allegedly arising from any information or suggestion in this book.

While the author has made every effort to provide accurate telephone numbers, Internet addresses, and other contact information at the time of publication, neither the publisher nor the author assumes any responsibility for errors, or for changes that occur after publication. Further, the publisher does not have any control over and does not assume any responsibility for author or third-party websites or their content.

To parents everywhere who want to make parenting the best job they've ever had. And to their kids, who will be so proud to call them Mom and Dad.

CONTENTS

INTRODUCTION

....

Long before this book came to be, there were times when I felt like the worst parent in history. One particularly memorable instance came at the end of yet another rough day, in a string of rough days, with my two young boys. My throat was scratchy.

"Great," I thought. "Now I'm coming down with a head cold *and* I'll have to figure out a way to convince the boys to go to bed without eighteen stories and forty-five drinks of water!" I wondered how it came to be that I, who for my career had effectively trained large groups of people, couldn't get my own two small children to do what I'd asked without becoming a complete ogre.

And then, as I raised my voice to yell at one of the boys *again*, probably for not picking up his toys as I'd asked him to or something monumental like that, a thought came crashing into my head and stopped me in my tracks. My throat wasn't sore from a virus. It hurt because I'd been yelling so much.

Now I was really sick. Could this be me? I'd always hated the idea of yelling at my kids, and here I was, raising my voice on a daily—sometimes hourly—basis. Why was it so hard for me to parent two very typical preschoolers? And what would happen as they got older and we had to navigate issues trickier than bathtime and table manners? I'd pictured standing by my sons' sides as they grew, and developing a respectful and communicative relationship with them, not being the person they put up with simply because I'd given birth to them—but I knew in my heart which track I was on. I felt utterly defeated in the most important job of my life. I wanted a big change.

That night, I asked myself the tough question: I couldn't possibly love these two kids more, so why did I yell at them when I knew in my heart it was the wrong thing to do? My efforts to "demand compliance" fell on deaf ears, and the "time-out" and "counting 1-2-3" strategies didn't work after the first few times. It seemed that there was nothing left but to raise my voice—at least they'd know I was serious. And so I religiously followed the vicious cycle of ask, remind, repeat, remind, repeat, explode.

I realized I'd turned into *that* parent—the one we all swear we'll never become.

Maybe you're familiar with *that* parent, too: the mom who bribes her 3-year-old with candy and toys just to make it through the grocery store. The dad whose 5-year-old has disrupted an entire restaurant with her insistence on skipping laps around the family's table. Or even the duo who takes turns cleaning the kids' rooms for them every Saturday morning because they can't figure out how to get their 8- and 10-year-olds to pick up after themselves.

We see *that* parent everywhere. Before we have our own kids, we get really annoyed with *that* parent—the one who can't control their own child. "When we're parents," we promise ourselves, "we will do better." After all, how hard can it be?

And then a year or two after we bring a bundle of joy into this world, we become *that* parent. We yell, threaten, remind, beg and finally give in, all in an effort to control our little cherubs. On our best days, we walk on eggshells, relying on little more than luck when it comes to ensuring good behavior from our kids. On our worst days, we turn into monsters ourselves and consider boarding preschool for our "terrible 2-year-old."

Without the right tools to get the job done, parenting is no longer fun. And that's sadder than a 7-year-old who really, truly is the *only* kid in the *entire* world who doesn't own the latest space dinosaur action figure (or whatever).

The problem is, we've always known what we *don't* want to be as a parent, but we have no idea how to be the parent we *do* want to be. And we resort to *that* parent's tactics because, well, they *must* work if so many parents rely on them! And sometimes we just have to get the grocery shopping done no matter what it takes. But in reality, *that* parent's tactics are only quick fixes—if that—and they don't work any better for anyone else than they do for you.

You've heard the first part of my story, now let me tell you how I turned my parenting style on its head—and made a huge, positive difference in my household in just a couple of weeks.

After that night—the one when I resolved to stop all the yelling—I realized that there had to be a better way. Inspired, I admit, by George on *Seinfeld,* I felt that "if everything I've done is wrong, then the opposite must be right." I enrolled in a parenting class that focused on positive parenting principles brought to life by early-twentieth-century medical doctor and psychologist Alfred Adler.

My world changed completely. When I began to implement Adlerian principles in my family, things started to get better very quickly. And the more I used Adler's theories, the more pleasant and cooperative family life became. My kids were happier, I was happier and my relationship with my husband was stronger.

I continued studying, and realized that while these principles sounded very good, a lot of parents were left saying, "That's interesting. Now what do I do?" There was still a need to translate the theories into a step-by-step, easy-to-implement process that parents everywhere could use in their own families.

I wanted to help other parents find the peace that my family and I enjoyed, so I employed my background in developing training programs in Fortune 500 companies along with my Positive Discipline certification to create my own parenting course, Positive Parenting Solutions. *If I Have to Tell You One More Time* is born of this parenting course, which has already changed the lives of thousands of families worldwide.

I wrote this book to give you the ability to manage the frustrating misbehaviors you see in your kids, and replace them with positive actions that will endure for a lifetime. I want to help you regain a sense of control of your family life so you can empower your children to learn the lessons and behaviors they'll need for future success.

Each chapter holds a wealth of psychologically grounded

information, examples and strategies for addressing misbehavior, including how to train your kids in positive behavior. But at the heart of the book are 23 Positive Discipline tools that include specific, step-by-step guidelines for directly applying the principles you'll learn. There's no more guesswork—you'll soon know exactly how to handle just about any misbehavior your children can dream up.

You'll learn how to eliminate annoying misbehaviors such as whining, negotiating, not listening and interrupting. You'll also learn how to ward off power struggles and temper tantrums, or stop them in their tracks. You'll be able to get your kids to brush their teeth, remember their lunchboxes and do their homework without reminding, yelling or arguing. And you'll discover ways to improve family dynamics, from fostering healthy sibling relationships to promoting togetherness.

If you find you've become the parent you never wanted to be, please read this book. Use the tools in your own home. One day, you'll look up and realize it's been a few days since you've raised your voice at your kids, or bribed, negotiated or badgered them to do something. And pretty soon, you won't remember the last time you yelled, reminded, begged or treated your kids with anything but respect. You'll smile as you realize that you've gotten the same respect in return.

Best of all, your world is going to change, just like it has for thousands of parents around the globe. Parenting stress will be replaced with parenting peace. You're going to spend more time enjoying your kids, marveling at how independent and self-sufficient they've become right before your eyes. You'll be amazed at how they graciously cooperate without eye-rolling or complaining, work out their own disagreements with their siblings, and complete household tasks without needing so much as a reminder. Of course, they'll still be your kids, and the occasional misbehavior will still pop up, but you'll finally have the tools you need to address the misbehavior and help them succeed in family life and beyond.

My suggestion is to read this book from start to finish, and put each tool to use as you come to it. Life will be better for you within the first few days of implementing the first tool, and you'll continue to see improvement with each new tool you introduce into your home. Then, since it'll take some time and practice to change lifelong habits (the ones, like yelling, that aren't working so well right now anyway), go back and read the book slowly, one chapter at a time, as a refresher. After that, you may find yourself picking up this book every few weeks as your kids grow and develop the propensity for new behaviors, both positive and negative.

I'll leave you with one final thought. When your kids are grown, how would you like for them to remember their childhood? As a time when any mistake or misbehavior was met with yelling, nagging and threats? Or as a time when they were taught appropriate behavior by a mom and dad who were calm and relaxed, within a family that just loved being together?

Join me in giving your kids the best childhood they could possibly dream of. Join me in preparing them to be successful adults. Join me in *loving* the hardest job you've ever had—being a wonderful parent.

If I
HAVE to
TELL *You*
ONE
MORE
TIME...

SOMETHING'S NOT WORKING

The living room is so quiet you can hear the clock tick. *Tick. Tick. Tick.* The tiny, rhythmic sound would be peaceful, if it weren't for one thing: You're waiting. Mentally counting the seconds. You've just told your 8-year-old to do her homework (or turn off the TV, or get ready for school, or go upstairs for bed), and she hasn't responded. Five year-long seconds have gone by. You know she heard you. And now, for what seems like the eighty-fifth time today, you have to decide what to do.

Already weary from the ensuing battle, you lamely resort to repeating yourself. *This will never work,* taunts the voice inside your head as you speak your original request a little higher and a little louder.

And it doesn't. Your daughter continues dressing up the dolls she has scattered across the floor. *Tick. Tick. Tick.*

You add a threat that you know you'll regret later: No seeing friends this weekend unless she does what you ask. This garners the response of "In a few minutes."

And finally, all quiet in the house is shattered as you explode, yelling at the girl in your best "If I have to tell you one more time!" tone of voice. She finishes what she's doing and then calmly trudges off to do as she's told. Silence fills the room again, but there's no air of satisfaction to go with it.

Well, that's over. You got what you wanted. But did you? What happens the next time your child misbehaves, acts out, talks back, dawdles or ignores you? The remind-repeat-threaten-yell cycle will start all over again. You'll feel angry and frustrated that you had to resort to such tactics.

You've tried everything. Time-outs. Yelling. Reminding. Nagging. Taking away privileges. Counting to three. And none of them work. Like most parents, you're fed up. You're tired of asking your kids to do the same simple things again and again. You're sick of hearing your own voice. You ask yourself (and even the occasional coffee shop barista!): Why is it so difficult to get children to do what they're supposed to do?

AT TIMES you may not feel like it, but parents today are smarter and better equipped than ever before. We can readily discuss the merits of omega-3's, we interview pediatricians and preschool teachers in depth, and we even warmed our baby's wipes to comfort a tender little tushie. There's not a challenge we can't tackle with the help of the Internet, from natural remedies to soothe sunburn to how to sneak spinach onto pizza. We're pros at quick fixes and tricky maneuvers—as long as we don't have to convince our 10-year-old to empty the dishwasher.

You'd think we'd have the whole parenting thing figured out, too. But one look at the average parent's frustration level—whether brought on by siblings who can't go five minutes without arguing or a preschooler who flat-out refuses to put on clothes in the morning—shows us that most moms and dads need help with parenting, and fast.

What about you? Because you're reading this book, it's probably safe to assume that things could be better between you and your kids. You may face whining, temper tantrums and homework battles on a daily basis. Even though you love your kids more than anything in the world, there may be whole weeks you really don't enjoy being a parent. You might be at—or nearing—your wit's end. To add insult to injury, you're probably already working your hardest to put your household in order and raise respectful, responsible kids. And yet, all your hard work hasn't paid off. Your kids continue to misbehave despite all your best attempts.

The good news is that it's not just you. You'll probably take comfort in knowing that parents all across the country are experiencing the same thing. The better news is that there's help. There are lots of reasons for your children's misbehavior—from societal shifts to strategies you're probably using that are fundamentally flawed. Fortunately, by following the methods outlined in this book, you can employ a solution for each of your challenges, and your family life will get much better, and soon.

You'll find you can implement the techniques you need with more confidence and success if you first understand the basics. We'll start with an explanation of the difference between two fundamental parenting terms to set the stage for the strategies and techniques that follow.

Punishment Versus Discipline

Parents instinctively know that discipline is a necessary part of raising children. However, many parents and experts confuse *discipline* with *punishment,* using the two words interchangeably in reference to correcting misbehavior. In fact, their real meanings vary considerably. A short overview of the terms will help give you some insight into various parenting approaches, and what makes them work (or not).

When 4-year-old Emma throws lima beans at 2-year-old Benjamin during dinner, your first reaction is likely to jump straight into applying a *punishment.* You reason that if you answer her negative behavior with a negative response, she'll learn her behavior was wrong. She may be banished from the table, scolded harshly or forced to eat all the rest of the lima beans on her plate—plus Ben's as well. Punishment is something we've had ingrained in us since childhood, whether through fairy tales or in the schoolyard: A misdeed deserves a little bit of justice. The mis-doer needs to feel the effects of her wrongdoing, usually something to make her "pay," like a swat on the bottom or a hurtful remark. Of course, you'd never want to inflict actual harm on your child. But consciously or unconsciously, you want to sour the misbehavior for her so that she never wants to do it again. The problem with punishment, however, is that it puts the child in a mode of self-defense. Instead of learning from the misdeed, the child focuses her energy on avoiding future punishment. Punishments even promote lying—after all, what child would confess to an offense, knowing that she was only going to be punished?

Discipline, however, is a much more positive, not to mention effective, way of responding to misbehavior. The word comes from the Latin *discipulus,* which can be translated to mean a student, one who is learning, or a willing convert. Instead of administering punishment, which is simply a negative reaction to a negative behavior, we want to make good use of every misdeed, as well as hold the child accountable for her actions. Each time your kids act out, it's an opportunity to teach important life skills that will guide your miniature adults-in-training to live up to their potential as capable, contributing members of society. By disciplining your children with relevant consequences and accountability, you ensure they won't want to repeat their misbehavior—because you've allowed them to learn from it, and not because you scared the daylights out of them.

As you react to misbehaviors using the strategies and tools in this book, remember that you're training your kids for long-term good behavior and, ultimately, success as adults. It's your job, using appropriate discipline techniques, to encourage them to be willing converts to the skills they'll need to function responsibly. A well-disciplined child is a well-trained child, and negative punishments don't have a place in this system. While your children may not enjoy the discipline process, they can keep their self-respect: Discipline doesn't involve physical pain, humiliation or crippling guilt. Instead, as we'll discuss later on, you'll use consequences as positive learning tools—even when there are lima beans scattered across the room.

Now that we know about the concept of discipline, let's take a look at what kind of discipline doesn't work—and a few reasons why your kids don't behave, even when you're trying your hardest to make them.

"Where did we ever get the crazy idea that in order to make children do better, first we have to make them feel worse? Children do better when they feel better."—Jane Nelsen, Ed.D.

Changing Times Mean Changing Children

One of the most common complaints from parents today is "My kids just don't listen!" Moms and dads often tell me that when they were young, they knew to listen—or else—anytime a parent shot them the "look." So why isn't there an equivalent of the "look" today? Why would our best attempts at the "look" be more likely to meet with an eye roll than a child who jumps into action?

It's not that kids are different today. They have the same biological and emotional makeup as generations past, the same DNA. But they are raised in a new time, and a new environment, with unique social influences. These changes—many of which have happened in the past few decades—greatly influence how effective we are as parents.

Just take a look at kids' lives nowadays: With the information age in full force, children even in early elementary school are in constant contact with each other via social networking tools, namely cell phones and computers. They're bombarded with what everyone else does, wears, buys or has. Children and parents hold to busy schedules, with little time left over for family or for kids just to be kids. And in the face of it all, there's more pressure on youth to succeed in academics, sports and the arts from an early age. In short, it's a lot harder being a kid today. Which makes it a lot harder to be a parent.

Sorry, Mom and Dad, but It *Is* a Democracy

As if blossoming technology and newfound pressures on kids aren't enough to throw a wrench into your plan of raising perfect children, another factor that's rarely discussed is how society and, as a result, parenting have changed over the last several generations. Our homes have followed the outside world in becoming a democracy—with as many opinions as there are seats around the dinner table.

This fundamental shift in control and relationships began outside the home, with governmental institutions, companies and organizations realizing that an aura of mutual respect is better for everyone than the authoritarian model of the past. For instance, it's hard to imagine a workplace environment in our society where a boss threatens an employee with "Have that report on my desk by the end of the day or you're fired." It's inconceivable to picture kids sitting at their schooldesks for hours on end learning reading, writing, math and history under the threat of corporal punishment or long minutes spent standing in the corner. It's laughable to imagine Dad ordering Mom to have dinner on the table when he walks through the door at six p.m.—or else. These scenarios would never fly today. Why? Because the norms of society and how we behave and interact with others have changed dramatically. The top-down, authoritarian approach to managing workers, teaching students and communicating with spouses isn't viewed as appropriate in today's society.

Instead, the workplace, the school and society in general are very different; they have moved in a more *democratic* direction. At work, input from employees is valued, actively solicited and considered at performance review time. A manager who continually harasses or yells at a staffer will be called to human resources, or even shown the door. Educators speak to children in respectful voices, corporal punishment is banned, and children participate in the learning process through projects and group activities. A teacher who hits or verbally abuses a child will be in the principal's office before you can say "Recess." The dictatorial "Do it because I said so" approach to education and to management is a thing of the past.

It's societal changes like these that have fostered how we parent today. They're the reason that the "look" or the "Because I said so" approach doesn't work with today's kids. And these relational shifts are a *good* thing. All of us benefit from a more democratic, respectful environment. This is the very atmosphere that will help us foster responsibility, kindness and success in our children. We can't do anything to change how things are for the sake of easier parenting, but if we really think about it, we wouldn't want to.

Let's examine home life in greater depth. Two generations ago, most families included a father who worked outside the home and a mother who stayed with the children. The husband provided the income and often made the rules, while the mother and children obediently followed. Husband and wife were not equal partners in marriage or when it came to raising children. Dad's word was the final word—many of us can remember the fear that coursed through us when we heard the phrase "Wait until your father gets home."

Today, most families look very different. Often, both parents work outside the home. Most husbands and wives view marriage and parenthood as a partnership with equal contributions (financial and otherwise) and input into family decisions. The result is that both Mom and Dad can lead productive and fulfilling lives— whether at work or at home—and model healthy attitudes for their children.

With this system, though, parents frequently disagree in front of their children instead of behind closed doors. Children observe this behavior and quickly learn that they, too, can share a different opinion (usually not as diplomatically as their parents do!). After all, why should kids listen to their parents when their parents frequently seem not to listen to each other? No matter how responsibly Mom and Dad handle disagreements, children still see that they exist.

As observers who are even more sensitive to their environment than adults, children understand that Mom doesn't simply obey Dad's orders, or vice versa. They hear their teachers and coaches speaking to them and to one another respectfully. They *intuitively* comprehend that the norms of society are democratic. And so, when we demand compliance with the "Do it because I said so" or "Don't question me, young man" response, children instinctively see something wrong, or out of place, with that way of thinking. Kids quite naturally ask, "Why should I have do what *she* says?" or "Who made you the boss of me?"

Such responses infuriate parents. They think back to their childhoods and, fondly or not, remember how they would never cop that kind of an attitude with their parents. I hear all the time, "I would never talk to my parents the way my kids do to me. What's wrong with these kids today?"

So, is there something wrong with kids today? What's a parent to do when the strategies they probably grew up with, such as the "look" or "Because I said so," don't work?

With these changing times, discipline methods within the family unit are due for a major shift. Although an authoritarian parenting style worked when past generations were growing up, it just doesn't fly today.

Take note that just because the old strategies don't work doesn't mean that kids today are "bad" or "disrespectful." They simply have a different outlook. As inhabitants of a democratic society, they inherently sense the need to push back when family life gets too constraining. When Mom says, "You'll do it right now, young man," her son's immediate instinct is to push right back with an "Oh no I won't!" And guess what: For better or worse, he's learned it from you. And likely every other adult he comes into contact with on a regular basis.

Let's face the facts: Society isn't getting any less democratic. Debates over everything from the environment to vaccines surge across our airways—and our carpools. Individualism is at an all-time high, and the thirst for knowledge is unquenchable. It's an environment that's ripe to foster future success for our kids and their world. But it's up to us to help our children live up to their potential, to train them to live responsibly within our democratic society as contributing, respectful adults.

To effectively correct misbehavior and create harmonious, co-operative relationships with our children, we must learn to think, act and react in a more democratic, egalitarian direction. And there's no need to panic. Don't think for a moment that you will be giving up or losing your parental authority. Democracy in the family doesn't mean that every decision is up for a vote. Parents are still the parents, the guides and certainly the presidents of their families.

The Positive Parenting Solutions principles and tools in this book will help your family move in a more democratic direction. You'll learn respectful discipline methods that are far more effective than demanding compliance. You'll learn how to get your kids to listen—and to do what they're supposed to do—but without nagging, reminding, yelling or commanding. All this while building stronger relationships with your children, who are becoming more capable, independent, self-sufficient and responsible, right before your eyes.

So, what's not working about the way you parent?

The Tried-and-True Strategies That Are Anything But

Society is full of prescriptions for handling a child's misbehavior. There's no escaping nanny shows on television, running commentary from a well-meaning neighbor or the outspoken advice from your childless coworker every time he hears you talking to your 7-year-old's teacher on the phone. You've probably tried time-outs, counting 1-2-3, various forms of punishment and offering rewards to keep your kids in line. In fact, you may have stuck to these routines consistently, and administered them exactly as you've been told. These strategies may even seem to work for other parents you know. And they probably worked for you—for a while. So what's the problem?

Take heart: It's not you. It's also not your kids. There are very good reasons why some of the most popular parenting strategies fall short—and I can just about guarantee that the other parents who use them struggle as much as you do, whether they realize it or not. Each strategy is fundamentally flawed, teaching our kids things we don't want them to learn and taking the focus away from helping them make better decisions in the future. In the previous section, we discussed a few reasons why punishments don't work, and rewards will be covered later, in chapter 4. Let's look at the two other popular techniques individually for more insights.

The Time-Out: Why Its Time Is Up

It's hard to find a parent nowadays who hasn't used a time-out at one time or another. For many, it's a staple of the discipline diet in their household. The time-out is featured on just about every nanny show on television, as well as in books, magazines and other media. Part of the reason for the time-out's popularity could be attributed to the fact that it became the primary alternative to spanking once parents learned that physical punishment is hurtful emotionally as well as physically.

But the time-out's predominance as a parenting tactic doesn't guarantee it's actually effective in correcting misbehaviors long term. Instead, this tried-and-trusted tool has two fatal flaws that may explain why most parents fail to report long-term success with it:

1. Time-outs invite power struggles.
2. Time-outs neglect to teach important life lessons.

What does a time-out have to do with power struggles? After all, aren't they supposed to help defuse power struggles by separating a child from the situation? The problem arises when any strong-willed or spirited child is put onto the time-out chair (or in the naughty corner, or his room, or wherever the sentence is to be served) and expected to stay there for the prescribed period of time. Now the parent's job is to keep the child on the chair for the duration of the time-out, while the child's job is to try to escape. Each escape attempt adds fuel to the situation, exploding it far beyond the scope of the offense. A five-minute time-out turns into a fifty-minute ordeal that leaves parent and child bedraggled, with both parties likely forgetting what the problem was in the first place. Not to mention the fact that most of us don't allow this kind of time in our schedule for handling a simple misbehavior. No matter who "wins" the battle, everyone loses. At its best, the time-out becomes a meaningless game; and at its worst, the time-out disrupts the entire household.

The second problem with time-outs is that they merely represent a punishment, and not a teaching tool, meaning they don't do anything to correct behavior long term. Even compliant children who are willing to sit patiently in a time-out through its duration have most likely learned nothing by the end of it. After all, do you know any 4-year-olds—or 10-year-olds, for that matter—who really use the time-out chair to think about what they've done and plan to change their ways in the future? This is the root of why parents often find themselves applying time-outs on a daily basis: They don't solve the underlying problem. The child may eventually learn how to endure sitting on a chair for a few minutes (or how to wear Mom down enough to end the time-out prematurely), but not the important lessons she needs for acting responsibly next time. A more effective form of discipline would allow consequences and other life lessons to train kids to consider their future actions more carefully. We'll talk more about consequences and applying them to misbehavior in chapter 7.

It may help to think about a time-out from your kid's point of view. Eight-year-old Aiden is playing contentedly with his trains and his blocks. He's just finished building a fabulous tower, resplendent in reds and greens and blues, and twelve blocks tall, for his train to drive through. The track is a perfect large figure eight with two hills and a tunnel. He can't wait for the first trip around.

The dubious smells of leftover meatloaf and green beans waft through the door as Mom walks in. "Aiden, please put away all your toys, it's time for dinner," she instructs.

"But, Mom, I just finished putting together this tower!" he (admittedly) whines.

"It's dinnertime," Mom replies. "Your toys have to be put away and you need to come to the table and eat. Do it now."

"I'm not even hungry, I just want to play with my toys. Five more minutes?"

"I said no!" Mom exclaims.

And yet Aiden stands his ground. Until dinner is burning and Mom has had enough.

"That's it, time-out!" decides Mom. "Ten minutes in your chair."

Aiden trudges to his designated time-out chair and plops down on it. The second Mom turns her back while setting the table, he dashes over to his train. If only he can get the train around the track and through the tower—cool!

Mom, unfortunately, spots him out of the corner of her eye and is back on the scene in an instant.

"What are you doing out of time-out? I told you to stay there!" she exclaims.

And back into the chair Aiden goes.

Forty-three minutes later, Aiden has finally served his whole time-out. He did manage to get his train through the tower, but only after six tries. By the end of it, neither he nor his mother is much in the mood for now cold leftover meatloaf and green beans. The impressive tower is destroyed, and Aiden has learned only that the most effective way of escaping from the time-out chair is by creating a distraction using the family dog and a stray bit of meatloaf he managed to snatch.

Poor Aiden. All he wanted was a little more time to play with his trains. And poor Mom. All she wanted was to help Aiden learn to respect dinnertime rules. So if a time-out doesn't work, for either Mom or Aiden, what does? We'll talk more about alternative ways to handle situations like these in chapter 2 and the rest of the book.

Why You Can't Count on 1-2-3

Another popular parenting technique recommends counting as a way to put a stop to misbehavior, theoretically allowing the child time to correct her errant actions. This may work the first time, but soon you'll find yourself going past three and up to five, and then ten, and then one hundred (to be brutally honest), as your child learns to tune you out.

The main problem with the 1-2-3 technique is that instead of training your child to reconsider her actions, you're actually teaching her to ignore you multiple times before finally (if you're lucky) listening and obeying. The script goes something like this:

Mommy: "McKayla, please don't run off in the store. Come back here."

McKayla, age 3½, ignores Mommy.

Mommy: "McKayla, I'm going to count to three."

McKayla ignores Mommy.

Mommy: "One." *Long pause.*

McKayla ignores Mommy.

Mommy: "Two." *Long pause.*

McKayla ignores Mommy.

Mommy: "Two and a half." *Longer pause.*

McKayla starts to slowly head back to Mommy, having gained herself an extra few minutes of play, which happened to be enough time to pull the sparkly purple jump rope off the store's "summer fun" display.

Mommy: "Thr—" *Long pause.*

McKayla runs the rest of the way, Mommy having given her plenty of time to make it back successfully. The two share a big hug (after all, McKayla came back to Mommy before she finished saying "three") and McKayla is reminded not to run off again.

While you certainly need to give your child enough time to correct misbehavior or to respond to your reasonable requests, the 1-2-3 technique instead shows kids that immediate action is never necessary. They're actually rewarded by ignoring you for as long as possible.

TIME-OUTS and counting 1-2-3 represent two specific parenting strategies that don't work for fundamental reasons. If you've used these with discouraging results, there's no need to worry. Just ditch them, and read on. Even if they seem to work for you, I'd recommend against using them—neither will accomplish the goal of training your kids for adulthood.

While some strategies work better than others, there are other factors at play when it comes to your child's behavior—namely, you. Before you can expect positive changes from your children, you may need to evaluate your child's needs, your parenting style and your interactions—and possibly make some changes of your own.

KIDS ARE PEOPLE, TOO

No matter what kind of parenting struggles you're facing, help is on the way. In this chapter, we'll look at the two core emotional mainstays kids crave most from us, and how our interactions play a role. Most important, we'll introduce a fundamental, life-changing tool at the end of this chapter for you to implement right away. Let's get started. Very quickly, you will see some real improvement in your children's behavior, and your peace of mind.

What Are Kids Really Trying to Tell Us?

Take a look at the following scenarios.

ONE afternoon, as your kids are happily playing and you find yourself with a few spare minutes, you decide to call a friend on the phone for a little catch-up. As she's filling you in on her trip to the Grand Canyon, your 7-year-old daughter walks up and catches your eye.

"Mom, I need you," she says in an exaggerated whisper that you know she knows your friend can hear.

You signal one minute by holding up a finger. She wanders to the perimeter of the room and glares at you.

Ten seconds later, she's back: "Mom, I *really need* you now!"

You stop your conversation and respond, "Can't you see I'm on the phone? I'll help you when I get off."

She's back in no time and interrupts you again. This time you explode, *"What is it?"*

"Um . . . um . . . my Band-Aid is loose," she replies.

Completely exasperated, you say to your friend, "Let me deal with this crisis and I'll call you back later."

ANOTHER TIME, you're in the supermarket, picking up a few things so you can make dinner when you get home. Your 5-year-old son pulls at your sweater and asks for a candy bar.

Your heart sinks: You know what you're in for. Nevertheless, you tell him no, hoping the outcome will be different this time.

It's not. He begins to whine that he's "starving to death," and you offer him a single-serve box of raisins instead. This only infuriates him (if he wanted raisins, he would've asked for raisins!), and pretty soon he's on the floor having a full-fledged tantrum.

You watch other customers walk by; a few are clearly sympathetic, but the rest you know are silently calling your child a spoiled brat and judging your parenting (or lack thereof). Now all you want to do is get out of there—you decide ordering pizza tonight sounds like a really good idea, and you make your getaway.

WHAT happened? Your daughter is completely capable of putting a new Band-Aid on herself—and she knows it. Your son will not starve to death without that candy bar—and he knows it.

On the surface, the Band-Aid and the candy bar may seem to be the focus of these scenarios. In truth, there's a much deeper issue present. Through situations like these, kids are unknowingly trying to tell us what they really need, and parents are unknowingly misinterpreting their signals, playing directly into the misbehavior.

So, what's the deeper issue? What is your child really asking for when he demands a candy bar?

A Brief Psychology Lesson That Will Make All the Difference

We'll get back to the Band-Aid and candy bar in a minute, but first we need to delve into your child's mind for a look at what's really spurring her demands and misbehaviors. We'll go back more than a hundred years to examine an established theory in child psychology that has influenced society for the better since it was first introduced.

Around the same time Sigmund Freud was developing his work, psychologist and medical doctor Alfred Adler made a groundbreaking assertion: Children deserve dignity and respect.

Although most of us would agree with this today—if not always in practice—it was a new idea during the time of sweatshops and "children should be seen and not heard." And it became the basis of his work, setting the stage for responding to kids in a more positive way.

Three of Adler's principles developed from this belief will influence all the strategies in this book.

Premise 1: A Child's Primary Goal Is to Achieve Belonging and Significance

Once a child's most basic physical needs for food and shelter are met, he then craves these two fundamental emotional mainstays. But what do belonging and significance mean from a child's perspective? In terms of belonging, a child needs to know where he fits in, his place in the family, and how he's emotionally connected to other members. And to feel a sense of significance, he needs to perceive himself as being capable, making a difference through meaningful contributions to the family. Along with that, it's vital that he feel a sense of personal power. Put a little star next to this one in your mind. Every human has a basic need for power. If we don't get it in positive ways, we will resort to negative methods, which often result in some of the most frustrating behaviors our kids exhibit.

Premise 2: All Behavior Is Goal-Oriented

You know all the whining, badgering, talking back, interrupting and other misbehaviors your kids grace you with on a weekly basis? According to this premise, they're not random. Your child doesn't even know it, but she's on a mission to achieve the feelings of belonging and significance she longs for. Misbehavior isn't the actual problem—it's just a symptom of a deeper issue. If we address it, the misbehavior will disappear and our children will get what they need in a more positive way.

Premise 3: A Misbehaving Child Is a Discouraged Child

Here, *discouraged* means that the child isn't getting a strong enough feeling of belonging and significance. When he throws a temper tantrum or clings to you, he's communicating something to the effect that "I really want to belong and feel significant, but I don't know how to do it." Your child is reaching out to you for help—he's not trying to misbehave, but he doesn't see a positive way to achieving his highest emotional needs.

When this kind of discouragement manifests itself in repeated misbehaviors, it could mean that the child errantly believes the negative behavior will help him accomplish his primary goals of belonging and significance, or in extreme cases, even more desperate goals. These instances are called the mistaken goals of misbehavior, and they are:

1. *Undue Attention.* A child whines, badgers, interrupts, clings, demands special service or acts helpless simply to get his parents' attention in a misapplied attempt to gain a sense of belonging.
2. *Power.* A child challenges or provokes a parent, with the goal of initiating a power struggle that she can "win," and in so doing, gain a sense of significance.
3. *Revenge.* A child has found he can't achieve a sense of belonging or significance, and instead just tries to get even with his parents by inflicting physical or emotional harm.

4. *Assumed Inadequacy.* Having failed in all previous goals, the child now gives up, detaches and wants to be left alone.

We'll cover each of these in more detail in chapter 8, but for now it's important to note that mistaken goals can be progressive (each one leads to the next, so as the child's discouragement deepens, Undue Attention leads to Power, and so on), and that they explain a real, underlying problem that needs to be addressed. You'll get the tools for doing so—or other recommendations—later on.

THINK of your child as wearing a giant sign around her neck—a sign that says "I want to belong, and I want to feel significant, but I don't know how to do it." But keep in mind that your child isn't aware of these needs of hers, or her errant methods for achieving them. She's simply using trial and error until she finds some way to get your attention or feel a sense of personal power. As parents, if we can give our kids a sense of belonging and significance in a positive way, we can prevent a lot of the misbehaviors that plague our households.

Keep these two emotional needs in mind throughout the rest of the book. They're behind every principle we'll discuss—as well as the tools that will start to make your life easier very soon.

Adlerian Psychology Applied

The concepts of Adlerian psychology tell us that when your daughter stops your phone conversation, she simply wants your complete and undivided attention. Unfortunately, she resorts to negative behaviors—nagging, interrupting and whining—to get it. Your son is bound and determined to gain a sense of significance and personal power by digging in his heels and doing the opposite of what you want.

Children have a built-in, hard-wired need for attention (a component of belonging) and power (which contributes to a feeling of significance). They're universal and non-negotiable—children must receive attention and power in some form, preferably positive. If they find themselves lacking in positive attention, they'll naturally resort to negative attention-seeking behaviors that are probably all too familiar to you, from whining to interrupting to acting helpless. They learn very early on that while they would rather have positive attention, negative attention is better than nothing.

Similarly, kids who are missing a sense of personal, positive power—the idea that they are capable, contribute to their families in meaningful ways and have some control over their lives—will resort to negative power-seeking behaviors to get it. This may be why you see back-talking, tantrums and ignoring your requests altogether among your children.

As another example, take the nightly bedtime battle.

As of 7:59 p.m., Daddy has just finished tucking 6-year-old Emma into bed. Already thinking about the big game just starting on TV downstairs, he's understandably not quite prepared for what Emma says next, with a sweet little yawn:

"One more story?"

Aw, what an angel. Who could resist reading this little princess one more bedtime story? Not Daddy.

"Sure, Pumpkin. How about Cinderella?"

Emma smiles and snuggles down under her covers as Daddy reads the story. The clock now reads 8:06, and Daddy gives Emma one last kiss and heads out the door. As he's leaving, he hears a tiny voice plead, "Can I have some water?"

"I'll bring you a drink," Daddy says, still enchanted but itching to be in his recliner. He gets the water.

As Daddy is leaving the room for the second time, Emma insists she's afraid of the dark. She sounds more awake than she was ten minutes ago.

Half an hour past when not-so-angelic-anymore Emma is supposed to be in dreamland, Daddy is finally fed up. And then the princess turns the bedtime battle into a full-blown warlike power struggle: She gets out of bed and turns on the light. All thoughts of cheering on a favorite team are shattered for Daddy as he tries one technique after another: insisting that she climb back into bed, warning her she'll be tired in school the next day and threatening her with an even earlier bedtime the following evening. Emma fights Daddy every step of the way.

DOES this sound like something that may happen in your family? The problem is, your daughter doesn't realize what she really wants: more time with you, and more power. As an emotionally mature adult who could articulate her feelings, she might tell you, "Dad, I just want you to spend more time with me and stay with me longer." But the truth is, your daughter is just a kid—she doesn't yet have the experience to interpret her true need. In fact, you probably don't often see this kind of discernment among your coworkers, your neighbors and even within yourself. Deciphering emotional needs is an advanced skill. And so, what started as a misunderstood cry for attention escalated into a full-blown power struggle, with your daughter determined to prove that she's the boss.

A child who deliberately ignores your requests to go to bed, brush his teeth, stop talking back, turn off the TV or anything else that's not particularly fun, is telling you that he doesn't like to be bossed around. Kids know that they have to go to bed, brush their teeth or stop watching TV at some point, so why do they act like this? Because they know that negative behavior will get your attention (even though it's negative) and fill their need for power (even though it's negative).

Life with children doesn't have to be this difficult. Parents can change the family dynamic by proactively giving children what they want and need—positive attention and positive power. Think of your child as having an attention basket and a power basket. The baskets have to be filled, one way or another. We can fill them up with positive attention, or we can provide ever-increasing doses of negative attention by continually responding to their whining, clinging, interruptions, helplessness and dawdling. We can proactively and intentionally provide positive power, or continue to fight battle after battle as our kids dig in their heels and become more and more determined to prove that "you're not the boss of me." What's more, we can do this without letting our kids rule the roost, and while training our kids for the next stage of their lives, whether they're age eight or eighteen.

These concepts are not intuitive to parents, but they're vital in transforming your children's misbehaviors into learning opportunities and keeping the peace in your house.

The goods news is that this book provides a step-by-step process that shows you how to use your kids' basic needs for positive attention and positive power to make a lasting difference for your family as a whole. You'll also learn how to stop those attention-seeking behaviors permanently and defuse power struggles in their tracks. Read on to see how other factors can contribute to a child's feeling of belonging and significance.

Birth Order Matters—But Should It?

You're probably already familiar with common birth order characteristics, and maybe you've seen them play out in your kids. We'll take a quick look at birth order, too—but as it applies to a child's feelings of belonging and significance. Not all children or all families are alike, but the following evaluations are generally found to be true.

Only Children

Because they're often the center of their parents' world, only children tend to have very high feelings of belonging. They're showered with attention and are confident of their place within their small family. However, their sense of significance can go either way. If only children are given their own responsibilities, a strong feeling of significance will come naturally to them. Then again, if they are coddled and everything is done for them, their sense of significance will be rather low. It all depends on the way an only child's parents interact with him or her.

Oldest Children

As with only children, a firstborn's sense of belonging is usually quite high. As their parents' only child for generally at least a year or two, and sometimes much longer, they have the opportunity to garner lots of attention and develop strong emotional connections, both of which contribute to fulfilling the core need of belonging. This can change, though, when the second child comes along, and the firstborn may feel dethroned by the amount of attention a newborn requires. In feelings of significance, firstborns also generally rate very highly. They're often given lots of responsibility, especially after subsequent children are born, and feel very capable and empowered.

Middle Children

Family dynamic really plays a big role in a middle child's feelings of belonging and significance. However, in general, middle children report a low sense of both belonging and significance. In terms of belonging, they often say that they feel somewhat invisible between the oldest, who garners so much of the parents' attention, and the youngest, who's the baby of the family and is also showered with attention. Feelings of significance, also, are low in middle children because the firstborn usually shoulders much of the responsibility, leaving less for subsequent kids. If you have one or more middle children, make sure you evaluate how their sense of belonging and significance measures up, and then work to distribute attention and responsibilities accordingly.

Youngest Children

Your youngest child is likely to feel a strong sense of belonging, which can be attributed to all the attention he receives as the "baby" of the family, regardless of his actual age. This could change, though, in larger families—if there are quite a few kids older than him, he could instead feel a bit ignored and have a lower sense of belonging. A youngest child's sense of significance is likely to be low because there is always someone who is bigger and more capable to step in.

With parents and older siblings to do everything for them, youngest children often aren't given much responsibility and don't develop skills that would serve to empower them and build their feeling of significance. You can remedy this by giving your youngest child plenty of opportunities to make meaningful contributions to the family.

REMEMBER that we want all of our kids to have a high sense of belonging and significance, whether they're an only child or number five out of seven. And all children are different—one oldest child is certainly not the same as another, since family dynamics vary so much.

As you evaluate each of your kids for their feelings of belonging and significance, consider the following from Alfred Adler: "The dangers of favoritism can hardly be stated too dramatically. Almost every discouragement in childhood springs from the feeling that someone else is preferred."

Of course, you'd never knowingly favor one child over another. But how do your children see it? Are you showering one with attention—for either positive or negative reasons—and leaving the other one in the background? Or are you handing one a lot of responsibility, which can be perceived by a child as both desirable and undesirable, and leaving the other ones out, possibly because their skills haven't developed as much?

To take this one step further and see how perceived favoritism can affect behavior, consider this from Rudolf Dreikurs, M.D., author of *Children: The Challenge*: "Children are expert observers but make many mistakes in interpreting what they observe."

For example, what does your firstborn observe when you bring her new little sister home from the hospital? The baby cries, and gets your attention. The baby dirties a diaper, and gets your attention. The baby complains of hunger, and gets your attention. Older Sister sees all this, but doesn't understand the intricacies of caring for a newborn and interprets the attention incorrectly. This is why you often see regressive behavior in an older sibling when a new baby comes into the house—she simply wants the same attention her little sister is receiving and assumes the best way to get that is to act more like the baby.

Your goal as a parent is to make sure all of your children, no matter their place in the birth order, feel a strong sense of belonging and a strong sense of significance. By carefully evaluating each child in your family, you can adjust your interactions and your family dynamic to foster these fundamental emotional needs in each child, reducing the misbehaviors that result from their misguided attempts to achieve belonging and significance with negative behaviors.

Parent and Child Interactions— The Three Ego States Explained

Belonging and significance are one piece of the parenting puzzle. Another important point to focus on is the way you interact with your children. In fact, it may only take small shifts in your communication style to transform your child's attitude from combative to cooperative. We'll begin exploring this possibility with another short psychology lesson.

The mind-sets we adopt as we interact with those around us are called the *ego states of personality*. They were first explained by Eric Berne in the 1950s and are still cited today. To put it simply: An ego state of personality is a mind-set behind our communication and our interactions. People have three ego states, which are displayed at various times: Parent, Adult and Child. By learning about them, you can gain more understanding about the interactions you have with your kids, and how they can impact a child's behavior.

Parent

In the Parent Ego State, we find ourselves being responsible for others, including our kids, elderly parents and even occasionally friends and coworkers. When we're communicating in the Parent Ego State, we're usually ordering, directing and correcting others with phrases like "It's time to clean your room," "Don't forget to take your medication," or "Just try one bite of your broccoli." It's our ingrained voice of authority, conditioned by years of listening to parents, teachers and coaches say these things. Do you sometimes feel like you're sounding just like your mother, or father? Well, you are!

Parents tend to spend the majority of their time communicating from the Parent Ego State. It's understandable, because we are responsible for our kids (or others), but this ego state brews power struggles—would you want someone hovering over you and telling you what to do all the time? When we order, correct and direct our kids or our spouses, it invokes a fight-or-flight response. Our kids can't flee, so they instinctively fight back.

If you're having problems with tantrums, talking back, not listening, negotiating every little thing, defiance, or other types of resistance when you're trying to get your child to do something, it's probably a clue that you're interacting too much from the Parent Ego State. The more time we spend in this ego state, ordering, correcting and directing, the more we can expect power struggles from our kids. To avoid power struggles, we should strive to spend no more than thirty percent of our time in the Parent Ego State. How much of your communication with your kids is currently spent ordering, correcting and directing?

Adult

As the least emotionally charged and most rational ego state, the Adult Ego State allows us to calmly and effectively share information and invite cooperation. It's the ego state you're most likely to operate from when you're at work or with other adults. Your child operates in the Adult Ego State while she's at school, as does her teacher. If you sometimes wonder why your children will pay attention at school but not at home, you can probably attribute their behavior to the Adult Ego State and the way it allows both parties to operate in an orderly fashion, with relatively few negative behaviors. However, it's interesting to note that if the teacher begins using the Parent Ego State instead, ordering, directing and correcting the students, chances are the classroom dynamic would deteriorate, with disruptions and power struggles becoming common.

Child

The Child Ego State is one of high emotion. In this ego state, we experience pure delight, impulsive reactions and exhilaration, from deep belly laughing to the pure joy of a child being immersed in something he loves to do. But there's also a negative side to the Child Ego State—meltdowns and temper tantrums (yes, even adults have them). Young children spend much of their time in this ego state—and hopefully the positive side of it—whereas adults, unfortunately, spend little time here.

Ego States Through Your Child's Eyes

Just as you react differently to the approaches people use with you (think about everyone from annoying coworkers to your best friends), your child will vary her reactions partly on the basis of the mind-set you adopt when communicating with her. Think about your ego state as you interact with your kids, and try operating more from the Adult or Child Ego States to evoke more positive responses.

CONSIDER your communication from your child's eyes.

In which ego state do our kids enjoy us most? The Child Ego State. Remember when laughing, enjoying life and having no cares in the world used to come so naturally? This is what our kids want from us more than anything else. We should be flattered—our children really want to be with us and have fun with us. In fact, the Child Ego State is the one in which the strongest emotional connections are made.

In which ego state do kids least enjoy us? The Parent Ego State. Too much ordering, correcting and directing almost always results in power struggles—and no wonder. Like anyone else, kids dislike being bossed around, and they tell us so with tantrums, back talk, arguing, negotiating and more.

In which ego state do parents spend most of their time? The Parent Ego State. *Hmmm . . .* that's a problem. Our kids want us in the Child Ego State. We spend most of our time in the Parent Ego State. This may give you some insight as to why you may find yourself frequently engaged in power struggles with your children.

FORTUNATELY, there's a way for everyone to be happy. Let's give our kids more of our time in the Child Ego State, where they really want us. Let's give ourselves kids who are more cooperative, with fewer power struggles. And let's give kids a power-packed dose of belonging and significance to build the strong, emotional connections that everyone is craving. It all happens by spending more time in the Child Ego State.

The Strategy
. . . .

1. Spend less time in the Parent Ego State. Be aware of ordering, correcting and directing.
2. Spend more time in the Child Ego State, using the first tool from the Toolbox—Mind, Body, & Soul Time (see page 35). It will feel strange to interact with your kids more often from the Child Ego State. But push out of your comfort zone—the results are worth it.
3. As you transition away from the Parent Ego State, experiment with the Adult Ego State and the Child Ego State to get the cooperative responses you want from your kids.

The Path to Positive Results

The Positive Parenting Solutions program is laid out in a series of action steps called Toolbox Solutions, or tools, which are based on the information within each section or chapter. You'll start by learning and implementing tool #1. You will see concrete results within a day or two. Then, when you're ready, you'll move forward and add tool #2 (found at the end of chapter 3). Each tool in the Toolbox builds on the previous one, with visible results every step of the way.

The best way to spend more time in the Child Ego State and at the same time meet your child's need for belonging and significance is to use tool #1: Mind, Body & Soul Time. As the most important tool in your Positive Parenting Solutions Toolbox, it's a fundamental building block for everything else in this book. The sooner you begin, the sooner you'll see your child acting in more positive ways, and the sooner parenting will be fun again.

Mind, Body & Soul Time

The Tool Explained

Mind, Body & Soul Time is the most important tool in the Toolbox for giving your child the emotional connection he desperately wants and for increasing your child's feeling of belonging and significance. It's also the most effective means of reducing negative attention-seeking behaviors. You'll be amazed at the changes this simple yet powerful tool will bring to your relationship with your child in just a few days. At Positive Parenting Solutions, we receive e-mails and phone calls daily from parents who can't believe the differences in their child's behavior. What's more, parents often say that they quickly realize they get as much out of Mind, Body &

Soul Time as their kids do. It fills them up emotionally and allows them to pursue other activities—whether household tasks or their own hobbies—without feeling guilty for not paying attention to their children. Mind, Body & Soul Time is:

- Time spent *individually* with each child
- Being *emotionally available* to your child during this time
- Doing what *your child* wants to do
- Ten minutes, twice a day, from each parent or caregiver in the home

Feeling overwhelmed? Don't worry.

Does ten minutes, twice a day, with each child sound like a lot? Before you freak out, take heart. It's okay to start small—once a day is fine to begin. And read on to learn why this is *so* worth it and how you can turn activities you're already doing into the quality time your child needs.

It's important to recognize that Mind, Body & Soul Time is one-on-one time between parent and child (no siblings around), when you are 110 percent focused on that child. As you let your calls go to voice mail and ignore your chirping BlackBerry, you may find yourself vrooming trucks around the room with your preschooler, playing a round of Uno with your third-grader or helping your preteen find new songs on iTunes. No matter how your child wants to spend the time, be prepared to get into the Child Ego State and enter into his or her world—that's the point of Mind, Body & Soul Time.

You may already spend *plenty* of time with your children; however, the power of Mind, Body & Soul Time is that it makes us rethink *how* we spend time with our kids. Think about it: How often, even when you're with your children in body, do you find yourself absent in mind and soul? Are you mentally writing your presentation for the big meeting, or budgeting for the family vacation, or jotting down a grocery list? As you respond to your kids with halfhearted "mm-hmmms" and "uh-huhs" and "wow, cools," they know you're only half-focused on their cartwheels or Play-Doh sculptures. They resent that.

Children can sense the difference between quality time and quantity time. We may spend long hours running to the dry cleaner's, post office and grocery store with our kids, but that hardly counts as quality time. And they know it.

Mind, Body & Soul Time is the way to fill your child's attention basket throughout the day—even when he's not asking for your time—*proactively* and *positively*. When his attention basket is full to the brim, he won't seek attention with negative and undesirable behaviors.

When to Use It

- Every day
- At planned times during the day (right after breakfast, before bedtime, etc.—whenever you can block off ten minutes)
- At least twice a day, for at least ten minutes each time. It's fine to start with just once a day until you get into a rhythm. When

you see the results, you'll quickly want to move it to two times per day.

- Whenever you see the opportunity to turn a mundane activity (a car ride, bathtime) into quality time
- Whenever you can sense your child's attention and power basket is nearing empty

If you're tempted to do all your Mind, Body & Soul Time in one twenty-minute period, resist. This special time is like emotional nutrition. If you had breakfast but didn't eat again for the rest of the day, you'd be starving and pretty cranky by the end of the day. Just as our bodies need food and water throughout the day, our kids need to have their attention and power baskets filled regularly. Doing Mind, Body & Soul Time two times per day gives your kids two solid doses of what they want and need most from you.

How to Carve Out the Time You Need

Initially, Mind, Body & Soul Time may seem like a big investment. You may spend so much time dealing with misbehaviors and trying to get your kids to do what you ask that you don't feel able to devote your mind, body and soul to anything other than the television.

Fortunately, once you consistently implement Mind, Body & Soul Time, you'll see the attention-seeking behaviors that probably plague your household begin to fade away. In fact, investing in Mind, Body & Soul Time will help free up your day because you will spend far less time hassling over frustrating misbehaviors.

Especially if you have several kids, though, twenty minutes a day per child can still seem like a big chunk of time. So here are three steps to making Mind, Body & Soul Time work with your already too-busy schedule.

1. *Steal time from doing things that aren't absolutely necessary.* Use it as an excuse to shun housework, or cut down on your own time on Facebook. After all, your child only wants to have fun with you—which can be, well, fun! Try it, and you'll be amazed how quickly you get the ten minutes back tenfold in good behavior.

2. *Find ways to make the ordinary routines and tasks more extraordinary.* Are there things you're already doing that you can make more special to your child? In the morning, stagger the wake-up times for your children so you can snuggle together with stories, songs, talking about the day ahead—or a spur-of-the-moment pillow fight. For a younger child, take a few extra minutes during bathtime to actually play with her, following her lead with her favorite water toys. Bedtime and car rides offer similar opportunities. Focus on turning your daily tasks into quality time, and you'll find that not only do you get your work done (albeit a bit slowly), but you'll give your child the dose of positive attention she really needs.

3. *Be consistent.* Set aside ten minutes, twice each day, for Mind, Body & Soul Time within your regular routine. The more Mind, Body & Soul Time becomes part of your daily schedule, the more likely you'll be to do it. Best of all, your kids will know they can count on it, without having to badger you for attention. Kids crave routines and consistency, and will soon take comfort in the familiarity of established special times each day, rewarding you with good behavior.

Why It Works

Mind, Body & Soul Time works by providing two of a child's most intrinsic emotional needs: belonging and significance. During the ten minutes of uninterrupted time, he has you all to himself and doesn't have to compete with anyone or anything for your attention. You're making strong emotional connections, reinforcing how important he is to you and filling his attention basket with plenty of positive attention. Because you allow him to choose the activity, your child feels a sense of positive power in having some control over his life.

There is a direct relationship between time invested in Mind, Body & Soul Time and behavior. When we invest in one-on-one special time with our kids, the return on that investment will manifest itself through a reduction in attention-seeking behaviors and power struggles, and an increase in cooperation. If we don't make the investment in Mind, Body & Soul Time, we're going to spend *at least* the same amount of time, but usually more, dealing with negative behaviors such as whining, tantrums and power struggles.

Missing out on Mind, Body & Soul Time means you're setting the stage for misbehavior in younger children, and emotional withdrawal in adolescents. After all, if Mom and Dad won't pay attention as you count to a hundred, you're pretty confident they'll be all yours if you decide to ride your tricycle down the stairs. And as a young teen, would you want to hang out with a parent who you know is lending only half an ear? When kids of all ages understand we're really making an effort to get into their world, they're sure to reach out, too.

The wise choice is clearly to give our kids what they really need: time with us in the Child Ego State, when we're giving them posi-

tive attention and personal power, and fostering their sense of belonging and significance.

Tips for Success

- Turn off the distractions. No television, PDAs, cell phones and
  the like.
- Go face-to-face. Generally speaking, Mind, Body & Soul Time
  should be an eye-to-eye activity that doesn't involve the TV or
  video games. However, for older kids, playing a round of Wii
  tennis may be the best way to connect with them in the Child
  Ego State—as long as you're not passively watching TV.
- Label your special time together. Before you begin, say, "Now
  it's time for our Mind, Body & Soul Time" (or Special Time,
  Mommy and Joey Time, or Daddy and Jenny Time). Labeling
  allows you to "get credit" in your child's mind that you filled
  her attention and power baskets in positive ways, whether the
  time you spend together is a scheduled Mind, Body & Soul
  Time or spur-of-the-moment, such as in the car.
- Label your special time again when it's over. Remind your child
  how much you enjoyed the special time together (calling it by
  your specific label) and how you can't wait to do it again tomorrow. "I loved having Mind, Body & Soul Time with you this
  morning and can't wait until we can do it again tonight."
- If it seems that finding an activity takes up too much of your
  Mind, Body & Soul Time, suggest that your child make a list of
  things that you can do during your next time together. Or, you
  can suggest an activity. It might sound like this: "I have ten
  minutes before I have to leave for work and would love to do
  our Daddy and Sophie Time. What book would you like to read
  together?"

QUICK-START GUIDE

- Identify one ten-minute block of time you can spend with each child per day, starting tomorrow. (You can gradually work up to two times per day.)
- Let your kids know that you're going to start doing something new that you're both going to love. Explain Mind, Body & Soul Time, and name it something that makes sense for both of you.
- Ask them to make a list (on paper or in their heads) of fun things you can do together in ten minutes. Offer a few ideas to get them started.
- Take the plunge! You'll soon be enjoying the time you spend, as well as the results.

FAQs

Since I have two kids who are close in age and like to do the same things, can I do Mind, Body & Soul Time with them together?

While the idea of spending time with both kids together is tempting for expediency, the answer is an unequivocal *no!* The purpose of Mind, Body & Soul Time is to provide a sense of individual attention and power to one child at a time. For those ten minutes, twice a day, your child will soon realize that he doesn't have to compete with *anyone or anything*—siblings, friends, your spouse, your work and other distractions—for your attention. He has you all to himself, doing what he wants to do for those ten minutes. What an amazing feeling of emotional connection and positive attention for a child! (By the way, there is an important connection between Mind, Body & Soul Time and sibling rivalry, which is discussed in chapter 9.)

What should we do for Mind, Body & Soul Time?
Think of Mind, Body & Soul Time as an eye-to-eye activity. It is something you play/do, but not TV or computer and preferably not video-game–based. The goal is to get into the child's world and do what he likes to do.

Sit down with your child and brainstorm a list of "fun things we can do in ten minutes" and keep it in a handy place. That way, your child can quickly pick something off the list for her special time and you can dig right in.

The no-video rule doesn't apply to kids who may be suspicious about your sudden interest in wanting to spend time with them. In this case, playing a video game together (not passively watching TV) can be a great way to start the Mind, Body & Soul Time process—they'll be pleasantly surprised that you are showing an interest in something they enjoy. Even if you're not an expert video gamer (or even close!), your child will be thrilled that you are trying to learn to do something she loves.

What if my child has a meltdown when Mind, Body & Soul Time is over?
This is a natural response when you start doing Mind, Body & Soul Time, especially with younger children, as many understandably don't want their time to end. They are also anxious that they may not get this special time again, so they'll want to prolong it as much as they can. To ease the transition, here are a few tips:

- Use a timer to indicate when Mind, Body & Soul Time is at an end. That way it's not Dad saying that we have to stop, but the timer telling your child it's time to move on.
- Have an activity—a puzzle, coloring, painting—planned for after special time. If you're going to prepare dinner, set it up in the kitchen so your child can still be close to you. If you're working in your home office, let your child play on the floor.
- Work to maintain consistency with your Mind, Body & Soul Time. Once your child is confident that she'll have that special time alone with you every day, at predictable times, transitions will be easier and anxiety will decrease.

My child has a hard time entertaining himself when it's his brother's turn for Mind, Body & Soul Time.

- Have Mind, Body & Soul Time with him first. Plan an interesting transition activity to engage him after his turn.
- While kids shouldn't spend a lot of time watching TV, this could be the fifteen-minute block of the day that you let him watch a favorite parent-approved television show or DVD while you spend Mind, Body & Soul Time with his sibling.
- Be encouraging when he does learn to patiently wait his turn: "I know it's hard to wait your turn, but you waited very patiently while I did Mind, Body & Soul Time with your brother. You are really growing up!"
- Stay consistent with Mind, Body & Soul Time for each child, even if it's tough at first. Eventually your kids will learn that this special time for themselves *and* their siblings is part of your daily routine.

I often travel for business during the week. How can I make up Mind, Body & Soul Time?

Use the weekends or any days that you're home to catch up on special time with each child. You may want to spend more than ten minutes twice a day with each child if you can. Many parents who travel during the week schedule dates with their kids on the weekend, taking a couple hours to go on a hike or work on a project together. While spending time as a family is important too, remember to give each child individual time and attention—they'll love every minute.

What if I want to spend more than ten minutes twice a day on this?

If you are able to spend more than the minimum time suggested, you'll be a hero in your kids' eyes! The minimum is ten minutes, but if you have time to play a more involved board game that takes thirty minutes, that's great.

What do you do if you have a large family?

If you have a large family and it's absolutely impossible to spend ten minutes twice a day with each child, then schedule your Mind, Body & Soul Time throughout the week on a calendar that everyone can see to make sure you give each of your kids their special time. In large families, it's easy for kids to feel that their attention baskets aren't being filled. Making Mind, Body & Soul Time part of your weekly routine ensures that everyone receives the attention they need.

My daughter thinks Mind, Body & Soul Time is "stupid" and "just for little kids." What should I do?

Your daughter probably isn't used to having this special time alone with you. Chances are that she feels confused by and a little uncomfortable with your new focus on her. Older children may also view Mind, Body & Soul Time as a ploy on your part to meddle, spy or pry. All it takes to get your daughter to open up to you is a little creativity. What do you enjoy doing together? Painting each other's nails? Baking a three-layer cake? Shooting hoops in the driveway?

Mind, Body & Soul Time is the first step toward permanently changing your child's behavior. You'll be amazed at the results you'll see in just two or three days. Your child will love and look forward to Mind, Body & Soul Time. And you will, too.

"Connection Before Correction" by Jane Nelson, Ed.D., author of Positive Discipline series of books.

ARE YOU MAKING YOUR CHILD'S BEHAVIOR WORSE?

A lot of factors can influence your children's propensity toward behavior (or misbehavior). From the previous chapter, you know what your child needs from you, and you have one strategy for providing positive attention and power to your child. Now it's time for a good long look at yourself—it could be that some of your child's misbehaviors could be abolished simply by making a few tweaks to your parenting style. It's worth a try, right?

In parenting circles today, we commonly remind one another of one basic fact: All kids are different. Whether we're discussing potty training or schoolwork, we know that our kids' personalities can make all the difference in how they approach a challenge, ask for help, handle frustration and measure success. What we often don't take into account, however, is our *own* personality—especially when it comes to parenting.

Let's face it, we adults are as varied as the children we parent. Some of us enjoy playing sports on the weekends, while others love nothing more than sipping wine while watching classic movies. Some of us are accountants, others are artists and still others are astronauts. We're silly or serious, straitlaced or free-thinking. We're Type A or Type B personalities, morning or evening people, optimists or pessimists, introverts or extroverts, and even cat people or dog people.

As parents, our natural tendencies vary as well. Many of us live up to the labels we have for each other: strict, permissive, scheduled, fun. We all react to our children's ups and downs differently, sometimes overreacting, sometimes underreacting, sometimes yelling when we shouldn't and sometimes laughing when we shouldn't (because little Caleb did just the perfect imitation of our spouse's "angry" face).

But it's important to remember that these natural tendencies of ours make a huge impression on our kids, especially when they're repeated over an entire childhood, day in and day out. So when our natural tendency, based on our own unique personality, is to ignore, or nag, or yell, or bribe, or whatever it is that we do to cope with our kids' misbehaviors, children are learning very important lessons. Unfortunately, what they sometimes learn are the very behaviors we're trying to combat, including whining, interrupting, tuning out, throwing tantrums and so forth.

Such an important truth bears repeating: The way we respond to our kids can influence their behavior, for better or worse. In fact, when I began studying Adlerian psychology and applying its principles in my own home, I found that about eighty percent of my kids' misbehaviors could be attributed to my own reactions to them. Parents who have taken my classes have reported similar findings.

Of course, that doesn't *excuse* misbehavior, but it does *explain* it. And if we can reasonably adjust our reactions to help our kids learn positive behavior, shouldn't we?

That's why our job is not an easy one. As the adults in the parent-child relationship, it's up to us to stop the cycle of misbehavior—and that often means changing our own behavior and the way we respond to our kids.

We certainly shouldn't alter our own personalities, but we can make a positive difference in our homes by taking charge of our natural tendencies, adjusting our expectations and measures of success, the things we work to control, and even the way we handle our children's happiness.

It begins by determining our own personality priorities. You can find yours by completing the quiz below.

The Parenting Personality Quiz*

What's your parenting personality priority? In other words, what personality tendencies are at work in the way you parent your kids? Answer the following questions with your gut response—don't think too hard about each one. If you spend more than three to five minutes answering these questions, you're thinking too much about the answer.

And be completely honest in your answers, as your results will

---

*Vivian Brault, M.A., founder of Directions.

help you determine where you may need to make adjustments when responding to your children. It's okay to be immodest—answer with "Most of the time" if that fits you. When considering statement 1, for instance, many people determine that they are capable of doing tasks better than most others, and that's just fine.

Also, don't limit your response to the way you parent—think of it more in terms of how you live your life most of the time. You may record your answers to this quiz on page 52.

Answer Key
A = Most of the time
B = Often
C = Sometimes
D = Almost never

1. I find I can do most tasks better than other people.
2. I prefer to do tasks that involve significant contributions.
3. I work hard, accomplishing much more than most people.
4. I try to be the best in whatever I choose to do.
5. It is very difficult for me to cope with failure.
6. I try to be perfect.
7. I usually know what is right or best.
8. I deserve special treatment.
9. I am always busy; I usually handle two or more projects at a time.
10. I am determined to see my plans carried out, and get things done.
11. I am a self-starter.
12. I try to make sure things are done right.
13. I don't like to be "out of control."

14. I try to get others to do what should be done.

15. I work best when I am boss.

16. I try to protect others.

17. I like to get praise from others.

18. I try to gain approval from people who are important to me.

19. I am sensitive to others' opinion of me.

20. I have difficulty saying no.

21. I do things for others when I don't want to, to avoid hurt feelings.

22. I let others have their way, even when I don't agree.

23. I don't like to interrupt my kids or bother others to do tasks that I can do for them.

24. I feel guilty when I say no to someone.

25. I have difficulty getting around to getting things done.

26. I don't volunteer to take responsibility.

27. I cannot handle stress.

28. I dislike it when people have expectations of me.

29. I do things to avoid dissention and conflict at home and work.

30. I try to get others to slow down and be comfortable.

31. I dislike being the boss for projects or activities.

32. I feel that in several areas, I am somewhat inadequate.

Answer Sheet

A = Most of the time   **B** = Often   **C** = Sometimes   **D** = Almost never

1. _____   17. _____
2. _____   18. _____
3. _____   19. _____
4. _____   20. _____
5. _____   21. _____
6. _____   22. _____
7. _____   23. _____
8. _____   24. _____
9. _____   25. _____
10. _____   26. _____
11. _____   27. _____
12. _____   28. _____
13. _____   29. _____
14. _____   30. _____
15. _____   31. _____
16. _____   32. _____

Scoring Instructions

1. Now that you are finished, create quadrants by drawing a line down the middle of the page and one across the page between numbers 8 and 9, and 24 and 25.

    You will have 4 quadrants:

    1–8   9–16   17–24   25–32

2. Assign a numerical value to each response.

    A = 4   **B** = 3   **C** = 2   **D** = 1

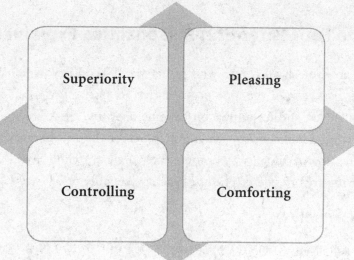

3. Add the numbers in each quadrant.
4. Identify the quadrant with the highest number and call it #1.
5. Identify the quadrant with the second highest number and call it #2.

   Quadrant #1 is your personality priority.

   Quadrant #2 is your secondary personality priority.

PARENT PERSONALITY PRIORITY RESULTS

My personality priority is: _____

My secondary personality priority is: _____

The Four Parenting Personalities Explained

By now you should know your primary and secondary personality priority. Each of the four priorities has its own set of assets and challenges, and it's important to remember that these are simply our natural tendencies—we can all overcome the drawbacks of our parenting personality to become the parent our child *needs*. Following are brief descriptions of each personality priority.

Superiority

If you have a Superiority personality priority, you're probably used to doing things in a "superior" way. Most things come fairly easily to you, and your history of achievement with most endeavors makes you quite self-assured in your own abilities. Modeling confidence and success, you demand perfection and set high expectations for yourself and others—however, sometimes unrealistically. When you respond to your children, you may often correct them and even lead them to feel incapable and uncertain in their own abilities. They may feel like they can never measure up to your expectations. Adults raised by "superior" parents often report that they were rarely encouraged as kids because the "superior" parent *expected* superior results.

Controlling

With a Controlling personality priority, you feel the need to be in control and you like things done a certain way. The corners must be wrinkle-free when your kids make their beds, and all dishes must be prewashed and then dried later on. On a positive note, you are comfortable making decisions and managing the aspects of your work or family life. In fact, you are likely an excellent role model for organization and leadership. However, because of your need to control the situation and have things done your way, you probably interact primarily from the Parent Ego State and tend to order, direct and correct others and be a bit rigid. This personality type invites power struggles with children and others. No one wants to be ordered, corrected and directed or bossed around, and when this happens, the natural reaction for your children is to fight back.

Pleasing

If you have a Pleasing personality priority, you may be fun to be with and have a lot of friends. Your need to keep people happy, however, leads you to avoid conflict, often by saying yes when you mean *no*, or by doing a task yourself that's someone else's responsibility. You are likely to remind your kids often about things they should remember for themselves, and you'll eventually resort to doing things for them. You may also find yourself giving in to their whining or complaining because you would rather avoid confrontation. As a result, you may end up feeling resentful and ignored.

Comforting

A Comforting personality priority means that you're probably easygoing as a parent. You go with the flow, without a lot of rules or limits. You probably don't like to hold to a routine, and you may be a bit permissive with your kids. Don't confuse *comforting* with *nurturing*, though. While all of the personality priorities can be nurturing, comforting here means allowing your kids to take the reins—appealing to their and your immediate happiness and comfort rather than long-term needs.

As you think about the four personality priorities, note both your primary and secondary priorities. For instance, parents with a primary Superiority personality priority often find that Controlling is their secondary type—which means that they expect a lot out of their kids and will control and direct them to make sure these expectations are met. You can imagine the impact this could have on a child, even into adulthood.

Keep in mind that one parenting style isn't better or worse than another, and each has its own benefits and drawbacks that need to be addressed. What's more, your personality priority is a gut reaction that often happens when you're stressed or angered. It wouldn't necessarily manifest itself when things are going well. In fact, we're more likely to temper our reactions at work, and respond with gut reactions at home with our children and spouses. This is why it's so important to be aware of your personality priority, and to recognize how your natural response to your kids might influence their behavior.

You should also remember that your personality priority is not an excuse for your own negative reactions to your child. Of course, we all make mistakes, but as responsible parents we need to continually strive to improve on our own parenting style. Even in the heat of the moment, *you have a choice*: Will you allow your gut reactions to lead you to respond in a negative way, and perpetuate misbehavior in your children, or will you adjust your reaction to promote positive interactions between yourself and your child?

The tools in the book will teach you how to adjust your reactions for a better outcome.

Making the Best of Your Personality Priority: How to Polish Your Parenting

By now, you may be thinking something like "Wait a minute. Before I change my kids, I need to change myself? This sounds like a lot of work!" Please don't put the book down—there's good news.

- If you simply make some small adjustments to your reactions, your kids will naturally start behaving better. You may even notice a difference in the way your spouse regards you.
- Although it may take a while for you to feel comfortable reacting in more positive ways, you'll probably see good results very soon.

Read on to find some tips for each personality priority for help in making the changes you need. And it's okay to start small: All the techniques in this book are meant to be practiced and used through an entire childhood. There's no quick fix to any parenting or misbehavior challenge, but even the slightest positive change will make a difference in your child's behavior, and also in the way you feel about yourself as a parent.

Superiority
- *Love unconditionally.* Make sure your children know that your affection is not based on their meeting your expectations.

- *Nix the negativity.* Recognize that even if your child doesn't accomplish a task the "right" way, trying his best is good enough. There's usually no need to criticize or correct.
- *Listen instead of lecture.* What's that old saying about having two ears and only one mouth?
- *Encourage effort.* Focus on movement toward the goal, including improvement and hard work, rather than the end goal. (You'll learn more about this method of encouragement in chapter 4.)
- *Let the children choose.* Value your kids' input and their ideas for solving problems and making age-appropriate decisions. Recognize that your ideas and answers aren't the only ones.
- *Give yourself some slack.* Just as your children don't need to be perfect all the time, neither do you!

Controlling

- *Ban the boss.* Limit ordering, correcting and directing—no one wants to be told what to do, when to do it and how to do it.
- *Quit correcting.* Don't insist on things being done your way.
- *Give up control, give choices.* Relinquish some of your own authority and let your child make lots of her own decisions throughout the day.
- *Relax!* Decide which issues are most important, and let some of the others go. If you choose your battles, there won't be nearly so many of them.
- *Become a "yes" mom or dad.* Turn a "no" into a "yes" with some simple rephrasing. For example, instead of saying, "No, we can't go to the park today, we don't have time," try "Wow, the park sounds like fun. We can go tomorrow after school or over the weekend. Which would you prefer?"

Pleasing

- *Just say no.* Remember that you don't have to say yes to every volunteer opportunity or request.
- *Just say no to your kids, too.* Your job is not to be their best friend. Instead, you need to balance kindness with firmness. Set limits and stick to them.
- *Let yourself be loved unconditionally.* Recognize that people—and especially your kids—love you and value you unconditionally. Their respect and affection is not based on how much you do for them.

Comforting

- *Root for routines.* Consistently follow them, for before school, after school and bedtime—plus any other times that are tricky throughout the day (such as meals or homework).
- *Balance tolerance with toughness.* Too much permissiveness may result in kids becoming demanding or spoiled.
- *Allow natural consequences to play out.* Establish logical consequences when appropriate and be sure to follow through. (You'll learn more about consequences in chapter 7.)

With your primary and secondary personality priorities in mind, practice the applicable techniques to begin to restore healthy expectations and limits for yourself and your child. It's okay if it feels strange at first. Over time, you'll find that these positive responses become second nature to you. Better yet, you'll find that positive reactions come more naturally to your kids as well.

OUR next tool, the Calm Voice, will help you temper your reactions to your children no matter what your parenting personality priority—because all parents occasionally get pushed to the brink. This tool is a method of positive communication that helps defuse and prevent power struggles, reduce stress and invite cooperation, whether in the heat of the moment or an everyday situation. It's a way to foster a more positive response from our children by making a change in the way you speak. It'll also help you interact more from the Adult Ego State. As with Mind, Body & Soul Time, you should see results within just a couple of days.

TOOLBOX SOLUTION #2

The Calm Voice

The Tool Explained

When you're a parent, every day can seem like one long communication challenge. How do you get through to frustrated kids who tune out your every word—or at least the ones you know they'd prefer not to hear? Are there ways to motivate your children without sounding like a drill sergeant? Is it possible to stop a meltdown without having one yourself?

The answer is simpler than you may think. While many parents resort to raising their voices to be heard over the chaos and to get kids to take action, being consciously aware of using your Calm Voice instead will actually yield better results. By controlling your instinct to yell or speak in the "I'm getting ready to lose it" tone of voice and instead employing a more relaxed pitch (even when you don't feel like it), you'll be amazed at how you can reduce the stress of the moment for yourself and your child, encourage cooperation and quiet a potentially explosive situation.

And by the way, I know that's not always easy. Sometimes our kids make us want to blow a gasket. But you'll come out ahead if you can manage to keep your calm—even if half an hour later you're sneaking into your parked car so you can let out the scream you bottled up earlier.

You'll also find that reducing the volume of your normal communications will help instill a sense of calm for you and your family. Think of Mr. Rogers, whose tranquil voice works almost as an enchantment to lull and relax children, while engaging them in his world. Many parents report that within just a week of using the Calm Voice regularly, their homes become quieter, more orderly, less intense and more enjoyable. You'll feel better about yourself, and your kids will be empowered to behave better.

When to Use It

Plan to use your Calm Voice all the time when you're around your kids. Your voice is a good indicator of your mood, and although you may feel the need to shout, yell or scream throughout the day, it's best for everyone if you can resist. Even in your everyday communications—whether you're getting the kids ready for school or taking them through the store—a quietly confident tone of voice will help instill a sense of security. Kids can easily sense your mood and will often pick it up themselves, so by speaking calmly in most situations, you can help your kids remain calm themselves.

Be extra careful to speak with your Calm Voice whenever you would normally feel the need to raise your voice, speak harshly or blow a gasket.

Why It Works

One of the reasons a Calm Voice is so effective is because children tend to mirror us. You've probably seen it from babyhood: Laughter is infectious, as is crying, as is fear. Although kids learn to temper their reactions a bit, the truth remains: We all take our cues from those who are important to us. While raising your voice only adds fuel to a difficult situation, when you reach out to your child with a Calm Voice and a respectful tone, he's likely to respond in the same way.

The Calm Voice is also the first step in making sure a power struggle doesn't escalate into a full-blown battle, so that you'll be able to spend your time helping your child make the best of the situation instead of dealing with a problem that's spun out of control. Children learn much more from our tone of voice than from our words, so in moments of anger and frustration, it's hard for them to focus on what exactly we're saying when they're overwhelmed by emotion. They may respond to tone, however, when words wouldn't get through.

What's more, using a Calm Voice will calm *you* down, or prevent you from getting worked up in the first place. And keeping your cool can go a long way in effectively handling a parenting challenge.

And last, but certainly not least, a Calm Voice empowers children to respond in an adult-like manner—which is exactly what you want them to learn. After all, you certainly can't expect a child to "be the adult" in a difficult communication situation if you're not doing so yourself. Instead, by speaking calmly and respectfully, you train your kids in a positive way to handle conflicts, disagreements and frustrations down the road.

The Calm Voice is a simple tool, but it wields a lot of power. In fact, it'll probably even make you feel better about your parenting—no one really enjoys yelling at their kids. The tips below will help you effectively put the Calm Voice to use with your family.

Tips for Success

- Start with sticky notes. It's not easy to begin implementing a Calm Voice. After all, you may have to change a lifetime of behavior—for both yourself and your children. A few sticky notes with "CV" or "Calm Voice" written on them will provide a visual reminder for you throughout the day—put them in your car, on your mirror, on the refrigerator and other places around your house.
- Ask your kids to help you. Let them know that you are working hard to use your Calm Voice and you need their help. They can give you a nonverbal signal when you are starting to get an angry tone or begin raising your voice. Not only will you score major points with your kids, but your whole family will be learning a more effective strategy for communication.
- Add a smile. Speaking with a smile on your face, even if it's fake, will help you maintain your Calm Voice and will calm others around you.

- Listen to yourself. As you begin implementing the Calm Voice tool in your household, start by working to become very aware of your tone of voice at all times. With practice, you can catch yourself ahead of time when you start to raise it or get frustrated.
- Pretend you're at work or at your book club. When you use the Calm Voice, you should sound respectful and composed, as if you're talking to a coworker or friend.
- Operate from the Adult Ego State. Remember our ego states? Make sure you don't slip and communicate from the Parent Ego State (ordering, directing and correcting) or the negative side of the Child Ego State (undergoing a meltdown yourself).
- Do expect good results. Many parents report that within several days of really implementing the Calm Voice, their children and family environment became much calmer and less chaotic than they were before.

FAQ

What happens when I blow it and raise my voice?
Don't beat yourself up. This is a work in progress and you will "fall off the wagon" from time to time. The important thing is to own up to it with your kids. For example, "I yelled at you because I was feeling angry about you leaving your dirty dishes on the counter and I had to clean them up. But I didn't handle that well. Instead of discussing it calmly, I flew off the handle. I'm sorry I raised my voice—it's something I'm working on controlling. Now let's talk about the situation of the dishes all over the counter."

BRINGING OUT THE BEST IN YOUR CHILD

A giant lives in 4-year-old Alexander's house. The giant has a voice that's loud and booming, with a stature that towers over Alex's 3½-foot, slender frame. This giant is smarter than Alex, stronger than Alex, quicker in thought and action, and unpredictable at times.

One evening, Alex plays with his dinosaurs and roars a little too loudly. "Keep it down in there," booms the giant. The boy forgets after a few minutes (after all, how many 4-year-olds can remember to "keep it down" when T. Rex and Stegosaurus are engaged in such a fierce battle?), and the giant stomps into the room. Wide-eyed, Alex looks up, up, all the way up at the giant's angry face as the giant lashes out. The giant's words string together and sound important, and Alex is intimidated once again into quiet. In fact, he decides to move upstairs to his room, a little farther away from the giant's reach.

While Alex does everything wrong, the giant, on the other hand, solves all the problems, comes up with all the answers and does everything right. The giant knows every detail about Alex and about the world, while most of Alex's knowledge is limited to the giant and the house they share. All day long, the giant directs Alex in a series of protocol and rules that Alex has never heard of, such as the fact that you can't wear red socks with green pants, and live worms don't belong on the coffee table. Impatient at Alex's confusion— and especially if Alex forgets a rule—the giant has a comment or suggestion for almost everything Alex does, and often a way to do it better.

As Alex fixes himself a bowl of cereal for breakfast one morning, some of it spills. "Here, I'll do that," the giant groans, yanking the bowl and cereal box out of Alex's hands. "You get the broom and sweep up this mess," commands the giant after the cereal is properly poured. "Not that way!" the giant roars as Alex accidentally dumps the spilled cereal out of the dustpan before reaching the trash can. "You're just making more of a mess. You go eat your cereal, I'll finish up." And Alex creeps over to the table and eats as fast as possible, shoving a piece of cereal that jumps off his spoon under the rug so the giant won't see.

Even worse: As if one giant isn't enough, there's also a mommy giant living here. And yet, Alex can't help but love them—after all, they're his parents.

THE GIANTS at Alex's house illustrate, from our kids' points of view, the inherent imbalance of power in the typical household, as well as how discouraging parents can be if we don't rein in our words, our actions and our temperament when interacting with our kids.

First, there's the sheer size difference between parents and children. In their youngest, most impressionable years, our kids aren't even half our height. Can you imagine the emotional impact of someone more than twice your size yelling at you?

And then there's the fact that we parents communicate competence to our kids. For the first part of their lives, they believe we know everything and can do anything—but they see themselves in an opposite light if we hold our capabilities over them.

What about the giant in you? Would you want such a giant moving into your house?

None of us feels good after yelling at our kids, and fortunately, we don't have to yell. There are gentler ways to train good behavior and get your point across to your children.

As YOUR children's mom or dad, you have a lot of say in what they think about themselves and how they assess their own capabilities. Your goal is to help them feel valued and included. This is different from making sure your kids are always happy, or perceive themselves to be "perfect"—this type of childhood would only lead to a narcissistic adulthood. Instead, you need to prepare them to become contributing members of society. And it all begins in your home.

Acting like a "capable giant" is discouraging enough, but there are other things we do to discourage our kids as well. And on a positive note, there are lots of ways we can encourage our kids. This chapter is dedicated to exploring ways to guide and motivate your kids toward *positive* actions, such as listening, helping and working hard. By encouraging good behavior, we can often head off misbe-havior and bring out the best in our kids. After all, isn't that what being a parent is all about?

First, let's look at a few more ways we discourage our kids—often without knowing it. Then, we'll move on to the good stuff—how to catch our kids "in the right," including a tool that will leave your child smiling from ear to ear.

The Ways We Discourage

Studies have reminded us time and time again that while people thrive in encouraging environments, they wilt in discouraging ones. Negativity is a powerful force that produces no positive re-sults, and for this reason, we want to ban discouragement in its various modes from our homes.

Discouragement, as you may remember from chapter 2, is the root of misbehavior: A misbehaving child is a discouraged child who is not feeling a strong sense of belonging and significance. A vicious cycle begins, in which a child acts out to boost his sense of belonging and significance, becomes discouraged again by his par-ents' response and, repeating this pattern, sinks lower and lower. As with many parenting foibles, we often don't realize we've dis-couraged our children until the damage is done.

We can put a stop to this cycle by using the encouraging phrases found in the Encouragement tool later in this chapter, and iden-tifying the ways in which we may discourage our children. Some of the more obvious types of discouragement come in the form of criticism, ridicule, humiliation or sarcasm. Certainly, we'd never knowingly adopt these attitudes with our children—not to mention our spouses, friends or coworkers—and expect positive results. However, sometimes we inadvertently do so anyway. Anytime we comment, "Is *that* what you're going to wear this morning?" or "Let's try to get the milk *in* the glass this time," we're being discouraging to our kids.

The more subtle forms of discouragement can be just as damaging. For instance, comparing a child to another is discouraging—whether you're telling Grandma with Jerome in earshot that he's a much better helper around the house than his older brother, or talking to the teacher about Colin's difficult day at school while he's standing right beside you.

Labeling is similarly discouraging. Would you want to be known as the "shy one" or the "clown"? Even seemingly positive labels tend to put kids "in their place," and heap on the pressure to make sure the label remains true. And simply talking about our kids in any kind of a detrimental light in front of them can be terribly discouraging.

Other subtle forms of discouragement convey to our children that we don't quite trust their judgment or their abilities. Whenever you jump in and help a child do a task he can do for himself, whether in the interest of time or because he's not doing it the way you would, you're undermining his capabilities and feelings of significance. If you overprotect your children by unnecessarily shouting "Be careful!" or "Don't go too fast" at the playground, you send them the message that you lack confidence in their skills. And reminding kids to say thank you or other things they already know to do garners eye rolls for a reason—not only do children need the opportunity to mess up from time to time, but they also need the chance to succeed without our help. All of these are discouraging because they assume the negative in your child—that he won't be able to figure out how to tie his shoes, that he'll fall off the slide if you don't warn him and that he'll forget to thank Mrs. Tucker after the playdate. Wouldn't you be discouraged, too, if the very people who train and encourage you one minute believe you're going to fail the next?

A final type of discouragement is to expect perfection out of your child. Kids can sense when we're more emotionally invested in their report card or cheerleading tryouts than they are. But the important thing to remember is that in order for your child to take pride in her accomplishments and learn from her setbacks, they need to be her own. After all, your daughter's good grades will get her into a good college—not you.

Rewards and Praise: The Most Subtle Discouragement

Two additional types of discouragement may surprise you, as many parents use them in an effort to promote positive actions. You've probably tried both: offering rewards to your child as motivation toward a behavior you want, and praising good behavior. Let's talk about rewards first.

You know the drill—when you want your children to behave a certain way, you dangle a treat in front of them like a carrot on a stick. You get to hunt down the items on your grocery list without also having to track a 3-year-old all over the store, and your child gets something he wants, too. Rewards can be as simple as an extra cookie for emptying the dishwasher after dinner, or as elaborate as a new bike for bringing home straight A's. Outside your home, you see rewards everywhere—stickers at the doctor's office for your kids, or a punch card at the coffee shop for you.

So, what's not to like? The real world is full of rewards, so why shouldn't you use them with your kids? Here's an example that may sound all too familiar.

TUESDAY is laundry day in 12-year-old Xavier's household. For the past twelve years, Mom has collected the clothes in Xavier's hamper every Tuesday morning, separated them, washed and dried them, folded them and returned them to his closet and drawers. On this particular Tuesday morning, Mom decides that it's high time for Xavier to lend a hand and learn to do his own laundry. But how do you convince a 12-year-old boy he needs to take responsibility for washing his clothes when he'd clearly rather be grass-staining them?

Just as many parents would, Mom figures that a small reward might work.

And it does! Xavier and his mom complete his laundry together. Xavier learns about wash cycles and how to fold a T-shirt, and Mom allows him an extra twenty minutes of video game time that evening. Both are satisfied with the new arrangement.

For the next few weeks, Xavier takes care of his own laundry every Tuesday, with help from Mom when he needs it (a previous night's "ketchup incident" was particularly challenging).

But then the resistance begins. As many shiny new toys and pet goldfish are well aware, it doesn't take long before anything that was once irresistible, and is now readily available, loses its luster. Xavier no longer thinks twenty minutes of video game time is worth the time and hassle of doing his own laundry.

Mom prods him into it for another few weeks, until Xavier badgers long and loud enough.

"Fine!" she says, tired of fighting. "We'll up your extra video game time to thirty minutes. Happy?"

Xavier is happy. That is, until the next week. Xavier and his mom hone their negotiating skills together Tuesday after Tuesday, until now, the expected reward includes forty-five minutes of extra video game time, plus candy as soon as his laundry is completed, plus a new baseball mitt if he launders his clothes five weeks in a row without complaining.

What's more, Xavier has now figured out that he can get payback for other good behaviors he had previously been demonstrating, such as putting away the toys in his room, setting the table and not picking on his sister in the car.

Mom must be asking herself why a little thing like getting her perfectly capable son to take on personal responsibility could spin so far out of control. Fortunately, there's a way to fix the problem: Stop rewarding. We'll soon go over some different strategies that will serve your family far better than offering payback.

Taken at face value, it would seem that nothing's wrong with using rewards as a tactic to motivate behavior. After all, don't we all appreciate a little payment for hard work? Of course. But problems arise as these incentives become expectations, and then demands. All of a sudden, it's not the parent holding the cards. Xavier has them all balled up in his tight little fist, and he's not letting go anytime soon.

The main reason that rewards don't work is that they're actually *discouraging toward future positive behavior*. While kids certainly enjoy rewards and they may seem to be effective the first few times you use them, kids soon learn to resist taking on a challenge, volunteering their service, excelling at school or work, or participating in almost anything unless they know what the payback is going to be. By giving your children rewards, you're essentially training them to demand "What's in it for me?" whenever they're asked to help out or put effort into something. It's an attitude that's difficult to grow out of—as kids grow and gain more personal freedom, they're increasingly able to demand payback for any project they take on. I don't think any of us want this for tomorrow's young adults.

Rewards can also be detrimental to a child's character. Studies have shown that children who are raised on rewards tend to be self-centered and materialistic. They feel entitled to receive rather than responsible to serve. In fact, these studies say that rewards don't actually motivate—instead, they cause children to lose interest in the positive behavior they were exhibiting. No wonder Xavier needed increasingly tempting rewards to complete the same task week after week.

One way to combat the feeling of entitlement that's running rampant in our society today is to make a clean break from rewards. That means no rewards for good behavior, and no payment for good grades or for helping out around the house. Later in this chapter and in the ones following, you'll learn the tools that really do work to inspire proper behavior from your child and hold them accountable for their actions.

We dangle goodies (from candy bars to sales commissions) in front of people in the same way that we train the family pet.
—Alfie Kohn, *Punished by Rewards*

Out with Chores, In with Family Contributions

There's a reason talking about money can be taboo—it's a tricky subject. And even more so when we're dealing with how, and whether, to give money to our kids. You know that it's not a good idea to offer money as a reward. But what about paying your children for chores, just as you get paid to work your job? That seems fair, doesn't it?

It may seem reasonable at first glance, but paying your kids to do chores around the house will only set them up for unrealistic expectations down the road and make it more difficult to engage their cooperation. After all, does a paycheck appear in your mailbox for all the laundry, cooking, cleaning and yard work you do?

Here's what Daniel Pink, author of the *New York Times* best-seller *Drive: The Surprising Truth about What Motivates Us,* has to say about the subject:

"This sends kids a clear (and clearly wrongheaded) message: In the absence of a payment, no self-respecting child would willingly set the table, empty the garbage, or make her own bed. . . . It converts a moral and familial obligation into just another commercial transaction—and teaches that the only reason to do a less-than-desirable task for your family is in exchange for payment."

As Daniel Pink points out, paying kids to do chores simply reinforces the negative lessons behind giving rewards—namely, the "I won't do this unless I get that" attitude. Instead, I encourage you to look at chores as "family contributions," and actually abolish the word *chore* from your vocabulary. While *chores* conveys a sense of drudgery, the term *family contributions* reminds children that the duties of running a house and making sure it operates smoothly belong to the whole family, since everyone also enjoys its privileges. While your kids still probably won't enjoy sweeping the floor or pulling weeds from the garden, they'll perceive these tasks differently because they'll know they're making meaningful contributions to the household. Through family contributions, each child will gain a sense of personal significance, as well as a feeling of belonging to a social group—namely, your family.

ANOTHER surprising source of discouragement is the praise we heap on our children for the good things they do. Here's a classic example.

IT's a big day for 5-year-old Kailey. Her soccer team is playing its first game of the season, and she's considered one of the star players—at least in her parents' eyes. Her coach, too, has let her know more than once that he's counting on her for at least one goal this game. He says it with a smile, and Kailey grins back with pride.

At breakfast, she's on cloud nine.

"How's my little soccer champ this morning?" Daddy asks over the special strawberry-mango power smoothies he's made.

"Great!" returns Kailey. "I can't wait! I'm going to make two goals, or maybe more!"

"That's my girl!" Daddy says.

By halftime, Kailey hasn't made a single goal. Neither has anyone else, but she's starting to get frustrated. She runs to her parents for a drink and a handful of raisins.

"Nice job, Kailey!" Mommy chirps as Kailey sits down.

"I haven't made a goal yet," Kailey moans.

"Don't worry, you will, you're the star player, remember?" Daddy reminds her.

"I don't know if I can do it," the girl says.

Coach calls her over, gathering the team for a pep talk. After a few general suggestions, mostly about "not clumping up around the ball," Coach turns to Kailey and takes her aside.

"Hey, Kailey, are you going to land me a goal today, Super Star?"

"Yup!" Kailey says bravely.

"Good girl! I know you can do it!"

The second half is worse than the first for Kailey. She stumbles around the field, kicks air and can't seem to follow the ball. Her parents ramp up their cheers, trying to help:

"Good going, Kailey! Good girl!" Daddy shouts with every kick in the right direction. But Kailey only gets more and more frustrated, to the point of giving up. Her team loses, 2–1, and she had nothing to do with the goal—she was sitting out trying to calm down at the time.

After the game, Kailey's parents remain upbeat despite the girl's downcast face. "You were awesome, honey. That other team just got lucky!" Mommy soothes.

"I hate soccer, I'm just no good at it," grumbles Kailey.

The family heads off to get some ice cream, but it looks like Kailey will need more than rainbow sherbet with sprinkles to brighten her mood.

THERE's obviously a problem here—but what's the issue? Kailey's seemingly ideal parents and coach may be unknowingly contributing to Kailey's frustration, and even her poor performance. What could they have done better?

Their big mistake was that they used *praise* in their well-meaning attempt to push Kailey to succeed. Kailey may have been having an off day, but wouldn't she have ended the game with a better attitude about the situation if she hadn't felt like she'd let everyone down by not acting as the "star player," as was expected? If she'd been encouraged about her hard work, her hustle and being a team player, instead of receiving praise for a goal she never scored, maybe she would've at least enjoyed her ice cream more once it was all over.

In the dictionary, the definition of praise is *to express favorable judgment.* Did you catch that? When you praise your children, you are judging them. You're putting yourself in a position of determining whether they're "good" or "bad." In Kailey's case, her parents were judging her as "good" or a "super star." But then what does that make her if she doesn't score a goal? Does she become "bad" or a "slacker"? Unfortunately, as most kids take everything literally, Kailey thinks that's exactly what happens. Other expressions of praise include phrases like "Good girl/boy," "You're so smart/cute," or "Great! That's just what I expected!" When you say these things, you do nothing to further your child's accomplishments—and you base their feelings of success on your own judgment.

The concept of praise became entrenched in our society as part of the self-esteem movement. We all thought that the more praise a child received, the better he would perform. Ironically, research has established that praise and self-esteem don't improve grades or career performance in the least (and at least one study says that meaningless praise can actually have an adverse effect on grades).

SINCE it's a type of reward, praise should be avoided for all the reasons we've already talked about. Like a reward, praise is discouraging. When you use it with your kids, you take the emphasis off the positive action (*the deed*), such as hard work, persistence or improvement, and instead make a judgment on your child (*the doer*). And if a child is judged as "The athletic one!" or "So smart!" she begins to be motivated by a need to maintain her label, or please her peers and superiors. For this reason, kids who are constantly praised are less likely to take on challenges for fear of failing—after all, why put in the effort if they just risk losing the approval of parents, teachers, coaches and others? They're also more distraught if they do fail, and less likely to view true accomplishments as such. Let's look at this concept in an example.

EDWARD, like any kid, has his ups and downs in the sixth grade. On his first history test, he brings home an A despite sitting up with a comic book instead of his textbook the night before.

"Great job! It just goes to show you're the smartest kid in the class!" his parents praise him when he shows them his grade.

A week later, Edward has a math exam; math is not his strong suit. Worried, he sits at the kitchen table all evening for several nights before the test, working on problems, occasionally asking

Mom or Dad for help. Whatever they can't figure out, he takes to his teacher after school.

When he gets his results—a perfectly respectable B—he couldn't be more ashamed. Would the "smartest kid in the class" bring home a B to his parents? Of course not, and he saw at least five or six A grades being passed back to other students. Edward hides his test in his backpack and hopes his parents forget to ask about it.

JUST as with Kailey in the earlier example, Edward's well-meaning parents focused praise on Edward himself. By calling him the "smartest kid in the class" for getting the top grade, they created a standard for him to live up to. What's more, they unknowingly endorsed the comic-book method of studying for a test by praising his grade rather than his (nonexistent, in this case) hard work, and potentially set the stage to discourage Edward from putting his best effort into studying for future exams. Because of the shallow praise Edward was offered for his history test, he didn't see his obvious success with his math test as such—he saw it as a failure. And what's more discouraging than that?

Even if Edward had earned a solid A on the math test, a simple "Great job—you're the smartest kid in the class" wouldn't have done justice to the work that he put in, which is what truly deserves recognition. By focusing on Edward and praising him as the "smartest," they could even imply that Edward doesn't need to work hard because he was born smart—he did nothing to manage his own success. That can be a discouraging concept to anyone. After all, we want to inspire our kids to work hard regardless of the outcome, and not simply to achieve a desired result.

Praise may sound good to your child in the short term, but it's still a judgment on your part. Kids who are praised learn to behave a certain way simply to gain your approval, and not because it's the right thing to do. While praise may seem to work for younger children, fast-forward ten years and you'll have a teenager who's no longer looking to you for your approval—she's seeking the counsel of her friends, whoever they may be. Teenagers raised on praise develop few long-term skills for deciding whether or not to cheat on a test or accept alcohol at a party. All they've learned is to go along with whatever the crowd wants in their pursuit of the admiration of others. As adults, they are at risk for becoming pleasers and approval junkies. And as employees, these grown-up children continue to demand praise and evaluations from their superiors, becoming high-maintenance workers in a world that's not set up to accommodate their many needs for recognition.

Now that we've talked about what *not* to do, it's time to take a look at what works. The next section and tool, which are all about encouragement, will give you a wonderful and effective strategy for fostering positive traits in your child.

Encouraging Good Behavior

What is it about parenthood that makes us utter fools for our kids? Why don't we hesitate to perform ridiculous stunts just to get our 3-year-old to laugh—in a crowded restaurant? How did we build such a tolerance for cleaning up snotty noses, and worse? And why is it that even those of us with the really challenging kids are just as proud of our 10-year-old terror as the parents of little angels are of their cherubs?

Science and studies aside, I believe that one reason is because we're in the privileged position of seeing the very best in our kids. We're their biggest spectators, and also their biggest fans, and nothing gives us more joy than seeing our children succeed and take pride in their accomplishments—no matter how big or little.

We're also our kids' coaches and trainers, though, and so it's up to us to help make sure the wins outnumber the losses when it comes to good behavior. It's in our kids'—and ours, and society's—best interest for them to learn how to act correctly in a variety of situations. Our houses run more smoothly, they do better in school and they're more prepared for life beyond childhood. So how do we inspire positive actions in our kids? We love it when they behave and succeed—what can we do to see that happen more often? First, let's take a look at the driving force behind our kids' actions.

Everything positive or negative our kids do is based on *motivation*. Motivation comes in two forms: external and internal. External motivation manifests itself through physical rewards and praise. People who are motivated by external factors are hoping to gain something tangible that they see as valuable (rewards) or gain the esteem of someone else (praise). External motivation always leaves a person dependent on someone or something else to keep them inspired or to validate their self-worth. Not only can approval and rewards be addicting, but they also lose their novelty, leaving the recipient wanting something more.

When someone is motivated internally, however, they look within for their reward: pride in a job well done, a feeling of accomplishment, personal enjoyment and other intangible emotions that aren't necessarily easy to come by, but are much more satisfying in the long term. Research tells us that internal motivation is the stronger of the two forms for these reasons.

When you look at your preschooler or young child, it may not seem to matter how they're motivated. After all, they have to learn the correct behavior in some way, and their attention spans are short enough that it may be difficult to get them to focus if there's not the promise of a cookie or a trip to the park to look forward to. But soon the 4-year-old will turn into a 14-year-old, with friends you don't know and long periods of time when you're not around to monitor her actions. When this happens, would you rather your daughter look toward the approval and "rewards" her peer group may offer her, or make decisions based on her internal compass? Let's help our kids foster internal motivation early on so that they're more confident in themselves—and their good decisions—down the road.

One of the most effective ways to do this is through Encouragement, our next tool. Use this tool to inspire positive actions and good character in your kids.

Encouragement

The Tool Explained

There's just about no greater way to empower your child in positive behavior, from helping out around the house to effectively leading a team in the math league, than through encouragement. As opposed to praise, which judges the child herself, encouragement is a carefully chosen expression that focuses on the positive behavior or character trait a child exhibits. It reinforces the action that led to success, and not the final result.

By tweaking each praising comment you're tempted to deliver and turning it instead into encouragement, you can help your child develop skills like hard work, perseverance, cooperation as part of a team, and creative problem solving that will lead him to success in all aspects of his life.

Here are a few ways to change praise into encouragement.

Instead of	Try
Good boy!	Thank you for helping me set the table.
Wow, another A in science!	Your hard work is really paying off!
I'm so proud of you!	You must feel really proud of yourself!
Great! That's just what I expected!	How do you feel about the game? Your grade on the project?

When to Use It

Every time you encourage your child, you reinforce that positive action in her mind, both directly, from the phrase you choose, and indirectly, through the positive attention you bestow on her. Use encouraging phrases:

- Whenever your child performs a positive action worth noting, whether it's spontaneous, like hugging a friend who's hurt, or something that she's been deliberately working on, such as a completing a science fair project
- When you're working to train a child in a specific positive behavior. For instance, if you're teaching your 3-year-old to clean up after herself at the table, encouragement will be a particularly effective tool.
- As a substitute when you would normally use praise

Why It Works

Unlike praise, words of encouragement reinforce effort and improvement, focusing on the hard work and personal achievement that went into an accomplishment, rather than on the child himself or the outcome. This puts the emphasis on important skills and qualities that will promote future success rather than simply on the end result.

The dictionary definition of *encouragement* reads "to inspire with courage; spur on." Practically speaking, encouragement inspires a child toward continued success by focusing on improvement and effort. Through encouragement, a child develops internal motivation for appropriate behavior, and also the ability to work hard at a task or challenge because he's fully satisfied in his effort. It's the idea that even if your kids are bringing home straight A's, or getting the lead role in every school play, or potty training in just one day, these accomplishments don't mean they're set for life and can quit working hard. Instead, while they can take pride directly in their own accomplishments—and even take pleasure in the accolades they'll no doubt receive at times—they'll also be able to apply the same lessons in working hard to achieve a goal to other situations down the road. They gain the confidence in their own abilities to assume that if one task they exerted themselves on went well, another might, too—and that it's also okay if it doesn't.

Encouragement also keeps the focus on your child in a positive way. Instead of judging your kids by telling them how proud of them *you* are, you can use encouragement to invite them to be proud of themselves. Remember, this whole parenting business isn't about you—it's about your child, and what they can make of themselves as they progress toward adulthood.

Tips for Success

- You don't need to make a huge change all at once. Pick one to three phrases from the list below to begin using whenever they're appropriate. Add a phrase or two every week.
- Get out the sticky notes again! Write encouraging phrases on them and put them in your car, on your mirror, etc. The more you're reminded of encouraging expressions, the more likely you will be to use them.
- It may take a while for your encouraging words to sound natural, and your kids may even get a bit suspicious. That's okay—keep working on it and soon they'll come easily as a part of your everyday language.
- Pay special attention to your kids' reactions. Chances are, they'll beam with pride as they hear you notice their effort, improvement and acts of kindness.

- Work on using encouragement with your spouse and your coworkers—everyone likes to be encouraged!
- Strive for improvement—not perfection—in your kids and in yourself as you learn these new tools.

Encouraging Phrases to Use with Your Child

The list of phrases below will help you see the types of expressions to use as you encourage your children, and the qualities to focus on. To get started, pick a couple phrases you feel like you could implement. As they begin to feel more natural, add to your repertoire.

"You must feel proud of yourself!"

"Wow, the floor is clean, the toys are put away!"

"You really seem to enjoy art."

"I see a very thorough job!"

"It's a pleasure to walk into this room."

"I love being with you."

"I really feel like we're a team when we work together like this."

"That's what I call *perseverance / leadership/ being a good friend*!"

"Very *creative*!"

"That's what I call *teamwork*!"

"Terrific effort!"

"That A represents a lot of hard work!"

"You're improving every week!"

"It looks like you put a lot of work into this."

"You really worked that out."

"That's coming along nicely."

"I can tell you spent a lot of time thinking this through."

"Your hard work is paying off."

"I trust your judgment."

"Now you've got the hang of it."

"That's a tough one, but you'll figure it out."

"You're right on track."

"I appreciate what you've done."

"Thanks for your help. That made my job easier."

"I really enjoyed our special time together today. I can't wait
to do it again tomorrow!"

"It's just like you to be so considerate of your friend's
feelings."

"I can tell you really care."

"How do you feel about it?"

"It must make you feel good that you planned ahead and got
everything done in time."*

How to Teach Kids About Money: The Allowance

In the previous sidebar (see pages 79–80), I recommended against
paying kids to complete routine tasks, or family contributions. However, it's still important to teach financial responsibility and money
sense. For this, I advocate giving your kids an allowance.

An allowance is one of the clearest win-win arrangements you
can offer your kids. Aside from the "cool" factor of getting money

*Adapted from Jane Nelsen, Ed.D., *Positive Discipline* (New York: Ballantine Books,
2006), p. 158–159.

every week from Mom and Dad, your children will feel grown-up and trusted. They'll learn real-life skills, such as how to make good decisions, and the consequences of bad ones. They'll come to understand the fundamentals of finance, including saving money for the things they really want, budgeting and investing. And finally, your kids will learn the valuable concept of delayed gratification.

For your part, you can cut down on whining and begging in the store by telling your kids to bring their wallets if they want to make purchases. And you no longer have to be the "bad guy" when your kids are nagging you for the latest gizmo all their friends have.

Recommendations for when to start an allowance and how much to provide differ, but whatever you decide, make sure that:

- The allowance is *not* tied to performing family contributions (or good grades, etc.). Kids need to contribute to the household because they live under your roof, and not for payment.
- Your kids know which expenses they'll be responsible for (e.g., entertainment, iTunes downloads and nonessential purchases at the store, such as candy and toys).
- Limits are set on what they can buy with their own money (e.g., video games must be rated E for Everyone).
- The amount you give isn't entirely comfortable—if your kids can almost always afford whatever they want, you're not teaching them anything. However, it should be enough to reasonably cover the expenses you're expecting them to take on.

- You encourage responsible financial behavior, including saving for the future and making charitable contributions.

Earn More by Doing More

Your children will naturally develop an urgent demand for more money at one time or another. When they do, you can then teach them about the value of hard work by offering extra, significant household tasks—beyond their regular family contributions—for pay. For example, you can "hire" your kids to dust window blinds, rake leaves or wax the car. Alternatively, kids can decide to put items they want on a wish list for their next birthday or for a major holiday.

With an allowance, your goal is to take the emphasis off rewarding good behavior, and instead put it on personal responsibility. Remember, an allowance is a training tool to help your kids learn about managing their own finances—it's not simply a way for them to fill up their iPod without having to wait until their birthdays. Teaching children good financial habits now will set them up for success in the future.

Encouragement in Action

Remember Kailey and her soccer game? Let's take another look at the story, this time with encouragement from her parents and coach substituted for praise.

It's a big day for 5-year-old Kailey. Her soccer team is playing its first game of the season, and she's considered one of the star players—at least in her parents' eyes. Her coach has been working with her on teamwork and hustling to the ball, and he's excited to see her progress.

At breakfast, she's on cloud nine.

"Are you excited for the big game?" Daddy asks over the special strawberry-mango power smoothies he's made.

"Yup!" returns Kailey. "I can't wait! I'm going to make two goals, or maybe more!"

"That would be cool—but what are you going to do out there on the field to try to make that happen?" Daddy replies, to get Kailey thinking about specific actions and skills instead of just the goal or outcome.

"I'm going to hustle!" she exclaims.

By halftime, Kailey hasn't made a single goal. Neither has anyone else, but she's starting to get frustrated. She runs to her parents for a drink and a handful of raisins.

"You are really hustling out there, Kailey!" Mommy says as Kailey sits down. She wants Kailey to see that hustling is part of a winning outcome so that even if Kailey hasn't scored a goal, she can feel good about her effort.

"I haven't made a goal yet," Kailey moans.

"Don't worry, keep working on the skills you've been practicing," Daddy encourages her.

"I don't know if I can do it," the girl says.

Coach calls her over, gathering the team for a pep talk. After a few general suggestions, mostly about "not clumping up around the ball," Coach turns to Kailey and takes her aside.

"Hey, Kailey, you're looking great out there! I appreciate the way you've been passing the ball to the open players on the field—that's what it's all about. If we stay focused on passing and being in the right positions, it'll be a great game!"

"Yup!" Kailey says bravely.

The second half is worse than the first for Kailey. She stumbles around the field, kicks air and can't seem to follow the ball. Her parents refocus their cheers to try to help.

"Good teamwork, Kailey!" Daddy shouts whenever she passes or receives the ball. But Kailey only gets more and more frustrated, to the point of giving up. Her team loses 2–1, but she had nothing to do with the goal—she was sitting out trying to calm down at the time.

After the game, Kailey's parents remain upbeat, despite the girl's downcast face. "I know you're disappointed about the game, sweetie, but from the sidelines I saw that your passing is really improving," Mommy soothes.

"What are *you* most proud of about the game?" asks Daddy.

"Well, I did feel like I was running pretty fast," Kailey admits. "I just couldn't kick it in the goal!"

"Is that something you'd like to work on? We can practice in the backyard!" Mommy suggests.

"Okay." Kailey almost smiles.

The family heads off to get some ice cream, and soon Kailey's chattering about her friends on the team over rainbow sherbet and sprinkles.

DID YOU notice how Kailey's parents used encouragement to set the stage for a more positive outcome whether Kailey scored a goal or not? Focusing on her improvement and effort, rather than piling on the pressure with praise, will help Kailey go into the next game with a good attitude and a can-do spirit.

EDWARD, too, would have benefited from a little encouragement from his parents. Here's his story as it might have played out if his parents had read this book:

EDWARD, like any kid, has his ups and downs in the sixth grade. On his first history test, he brings home an A despite sitting up with a comic book instead of his textbook the night before.

"Wow, you seem to really enjoy history," his parents remark, focusing on Edward's interest in the subject instead of labeling him as the "smartest in the class."

"Yup, I'm pretty good at it!" beams Edward in response, relieved that it looks like at least one class this year will be easy.

"There's a Civil War battle reenactment on Saturday that we could go to if you'd like," his parents reply, working to encourage his interest and inspire him to learn more rather than just coast.

"Um, sure!" agrees Edward.

A week later, Edward is faced with an upcoming math exam, and math isn't his strong suit. Worried, he sits at the kitchen table all evening for several nights before the test, working on problems, occasionally asking Mom or Dad for help. Whatever they can't figure out, he takes to his teacher after school.

The night before the test, Edward's parents offer a few words of encouragement: "I know you've been concerned about the math test this week," says Mom, "but it's obvious you are putting in a lot of hard work and using all your resources to learn the material."

"You should be really proud of yourself," Dad adds.

When Edward gets his results—a perfectly respectable B—he knows it pales in comparison to the A on the history test and is feeling a little down about the grade. Over dinner, his parents ask him how he did, and he simply replies, "I got a B."

His parents just nod. "How do you feel about your grade?" asks Dad.

"Well, pretty good—it was a really hard test," says Edward.

"I agree," says Mom with a smile. "That B is the result of a lot of study time on your part and going the extra mile to learn something that was challenging for you. Your B probably means more to you than the A you got last week on the history exam."

"That kind of hard work and perseverance is going to serve you well in the years to come—congratulations!" says Dad.

Edward grins, finally feeling proud of his accomplishment.

THROUGH encouragement from his parents, Edward begins to learn that it's the effort that counts—not necessarily the end result. What's more, he finds that his grade is only one measure of success, it's more important that he can be proud of giving it his all, whatever the challenge.

As one last example, take a look at how encouragement plays a role even in an everyday situation.

SOMEWHAT BORED, as 7-year-olds occasionally are, Josie wanders into the kitchen and finds her mom cooking dinner. "What are we having?" she predictably asks.

"Chicken and rice," her mother replies, busy with her preparations at the counter.

"Oh," says Josie, as bored as ever.

"Hey, would you please set the table for me?" Josie's mom asks, grateful for the promise of help.

"Sure," Josie replies, partly because she can't think of anything better to do. As she completes the task, her mom is able to finish the casserole and slide it into the oven to bake. Relieved that dinner and table-setting are now checked off her to-do list, she turns back to her daughter, who's halfheartedly flipping through the junk mail.

"Thanks so much for setting the table, sweetie. I really appreciate how you're always willing to lend a hand when asked!"

Josie smiles. Then she figures she might as well ask, "Can we play a game of Uno before dinner?"

Mom thinks for a second, and realizes she does have a few extra minutes while dinner bakes. "Sure, thanks to your help, now I have time for a hand or two! Let's get out the cards."

It's a win-win situation for both Josie and her mom. Mom gets her load lightened a bit, while Josie gets to see how her contributions directly help the family, making her feel significant. Both get to enjoy some time together while dinner bakes. And what do you think Josie will say next time Mom asks her to lend a hand? Encouragement can work just as well in your household, too.

THROUGH ENCOURAGEMENT, kids learn to assess their efforts and decisions on their own terms. And when your children are deciding whether to cheat on that test or accept a glass of beer from their friends, they can look to their internal compass for guidance, and be confident in making the right choice for themselves. When you think about it, the ability to eliminate the middleman and look only within for approval—and not to someone else—is truly a gift. Wouldn't we all have benefited from developing this skill throughout childhood?

It's not that you can never praise your child with a "good girl" or an "I'm proud of you." But praise is like candy. If your kids subsist on a diet of sugar and chocolate, they most likely won't grow into healthy adults. However, as long as most of their emotional nutrition comes in the form of encouragement, a few words of praise certainly won't hurt. For instance, as your daughter is dribbling down the court and going for a layup with five seconds left in the basketball game, there's no need to shout, "It must feel good when your hard work pays off like this!" Go ahead and cheer on your child with a "That's my girl! Way to go!" But on the way home, reinforce her hard work through encouragement. A simple "All that effort you put into practicing layups in the driveway is paying off! You should be really proud of yourself!" will teach her valuable lessons—and put a huge smile on her face.

Piggybacking: The Encouragement Killer

One especially subtle type of discouragement is often unrecognizable as such because it comes right on the heels of encouragement. Take a look at a few examples:

"Wow, you spent a lot of time cleaning your room. If only it could stay this way all the time!"

"Good thing you remembered your umbrella. But don't you wish you'd worn your boots like I told you?"

"Don't you feel better getting your homework done right away?"

———————

CAN you see what these phrases are doing? Our internal intent with piggybacking is to somehow prove that we're right—to show our kids that if they'd just listen to us all the time, they'd be much better off. We adopt an "I told you so" attitude. And it's just as annoying—not to mention discouraging—to our kids as it would be to us if our boss spoke that way. If we heard "This is great—for a start" every time we wrote up a report at work, it wouldn't be long before we quit giving our best effort.

In our children's eyes, piggybacking adds a sense of embarrassment or guilt to an otherwise positive statement. This shatters the pride and joy they felt about a job well done, and they go from delighted to deflated. Kids become angry and defensive at piggybacking—who wouldn't?

What makes us piggyback? What are we trying to accomplish? Most of us do it with the best intentions in the name of training, eager to hammer home a point. We want them to finally realize what a relief it is to get homework done right away or how much easier it is to find an inch-long plastic doll shoe in a clean room than a cluttered one. However, if we're not careful, we can make a wonderful, encouraging expression completely backfire. In truth, encouragement that stands alone is much more powerful than any piggyback point we add to it. Simple encouragement allows the child to own the hard work or the behavior that contributed to the positive outcome versus putting a child on the defensive with an "I told you so" remark.

There's an easy fix for piggybacking: Speak your encouraging phrase, and then close your mouth. You'll get your point across much better without a final zinger. What's more, you may find that this is something you can work on with others around you. Your spouse doesn't appreciate piggybacking any more than your children do.

As you practice encouraging phrases from the Encouragement Toolbox Solution earlier in the chapter, make sure you remember that they stand alone. Let your child revel in her accomplishment, and save the "I told you so" for your diary.

The Encouragement-Versus-Praise Quiz

It can be tricky, especially at first, to learn the difference between praise and encouragement. See if you're catching on using the quiz below. After each phrase, mark whether you think it's encouragement or praise. Then assess your quiz. For each answer, I've included a reason why it's encouragement or praise, as well as an alternative expression to use instead of praise.

1. "I'm so proud of you."
2. "I appreciate your help."
3. "Look at your improvement."
4. "You're the cutest."
5. "That A reflects a lot of hard work."
6. "You are such a good boy."
7. "You are so smart."
8. "I like the way Sara is sitting quietly."
9. "Look how far you've come."
10. "I love being with you."

Answer Key

PRAISE: Numbers 1, 4, 6, 7, 8

ENCOURAGEMENT: Numbers 2, 3, 5, 9, 10

Explanations

1. *I'm so proud of you.*

   PRAISE. The focus is on the parent being proud of the child, instead of the child being proud of himself. It's okay to be proud of your child and to communicate that, but it's more important that he develop internal motivation. We don't want him to behave in a certain way to please us; instead, we want him to work hard and do well because he feels proud of himself. When the child asks, "Are you proud of me?" you can respond by saying, "I am proud of you, but what's really important is that you are proud of yourself. How do you feel about your work?"

2. *I appreciate your help.*

   ENCOURAGEMENT. The focus is on the deed—the help. When we encourage the deed, it helps our children feel significant and they are more likely to repeat that behavior in the future. You can also add a comment about how the deed specifically helped, for instance, "I appreciate your help packing lunches this morning because it gave me a little extra time to get the kitchen cleaned up."

3. *Look at your improvement.*

   ENCOURAGEMENT. The focus is on the improvement. With encouragement, we're not focused on the end product, we're focused on progress toward the goal. Even the slightest bit of movement in the right direction can be encouraged. When we encourage the effort and the improvement, kids feel proud of themselves—even if they don't quite get to the goal.

4. *You're the cutest.*

   PRAISE. The focus is on external beauty and creates a need for external motivation. To be more encouraging, concentrate on your child's unique qualities on the inside.

5. *That A reflects a lot of hard work.*

   ENCOURAGEMENT. With this statement, we're tying the A to hard work. A's are nice, but we want to instill in our children that hard work will lead to results. Even if they work their hardest and bring home a B or C, the hard work is the most important thing.

6. *You are such a good boy.*

   PRAISE. The focus is on the doer, not the deed. "Good boy" is also a label. Anytime we are giving our kids a label, it puts pressure on them to always live up to that label. To be more encouraging, focus on the positive behavior your child is exhibiting:

   "Thank you for setting the table—that really helped me!"

   "I noticed how patient you were being with your brother."

   "You worked really hard getting this room clean!"

7. *You are so smart.*

   Big-time praise! Once again, even when we give a child a positive label such as "smart," we place a tremendous amount of pressure on her to always be "smart." Eventually, there will be subjects that don't come as easily—and how will your child feel when she is struggling? Will she share that with you? Perhaps she will take easier classes in a certain subject instead of really challenging herself—all to preserve her "smart" label. Instead of labeling the child "smart," focus on the enjoyment of learning and the qualities that will help her get through the difficult subjects she may meet with in the future:

"Your hard work is really paying off."

"You seem to really enjoy science."

"You are really improving."

More than three decades of research show that a focus on effort—not intelligence or ability—is key to success in school and in life.

Carol Dweck, Ph.D.

Mindset: The New Psychology of Success

8. *I like the way Sara is sitting quietly.*

PRAISE. Teachers are trained to use this technique to get a desired behavior from the class. Parents often do this between siblings. But drawing attention to Sara and the way she is sitting is discouraging to the rest of the class. Between siblings, when we point out to one child how the other one is doing something desirable, we are making discouraging comparisons. Instead of praising Sara, focus on the behavior you want to see:

At school: "When I see everyone sitting crisscross-applesauce with no talking, then we'll begin the story."

At home: "When everyone is sitting on their chairs with napkins on their laps, then we'll serve dinner."

9. *Look how far you've come.*

ENCOURAGEMENT. The focus is on improvement, and movement toward the goal.

10. *I love being with you.*

ENCOURAGEMENT. It's not about your grades or your performance on the field—I just love being with *you*. Expressing unconditional love is very encouraging.*

---

*Adapted from Lynn Lott & Jane Nelsen, Ph.D., *Parenting the Positive Discipline Way* Facilitators Manual.

A Final Note on Feeling Overwhelmed

Many parents tell me that after hearing all this information about the differences between praise and encouragement and the pitfalls of piggybacking, they're afraid to say anything at all to their kids. But take heart: No one expects you to flip a switch and become well-versed in encouraging phrases overnight. Work on making progress, not complete perfection. If you can make a majority of your words encouraging, and cut out a lot of the discouraging ones, you're doing great. Review the Encouragement Toolbox Solution for suggested phrases, and try to add a few to your vocabulary each week.

Pay special attention to your kids' reactions—you'll be able to see the personal pride written in their expressions. Using encouragement, you can positively impact your kids' behavior as well as the quality of relationship you have with them. And I think you'll agree that the effort on your part is worth the long-lasting returns.

THE POWER AND
THE STRUGGLE
(AND SOME SOLUTIONS)

Every morning at seven, 6-year-old Gabriel is woken up by his dad. Still drowsy-eyed, he's gently prodded to get dressed in the outfit his mom has laid out for him the night before. Today it's a red sweater that itches and jeans that he was once made fun of for because they're about two inches too short. Dad then makes sure he washes his face and brushes his hair. Downstairs at the breakfast table, Mom is pouring the milk on a bowl of Cheerios for him. She hands Gabriel a banana and reminds him to finish his orange juice quickly, because the bus will be here in ten minutes. Gabriel then is sent back upstairs to brush his teeth and gather his things. As he heads out the door for school, Mom puts a lunch bag into his hands and an umbrella into his backpack before holding out an old rain jacket for him. She smooths down Gabriel's hair as she reminds him that he has a piano lesson after school, so he should try not to get dirty on the playground and shouldn't invite any of his friends home from school. The last thing Gabriel hears before hopping onto the bus is an instruction to get milk for lunch, and not juice like he has been. He sneaks a peek into his lunch bag and sees that it's bologna again—not exactly Gabriel's favorite. And his mom forgot to include the fruit snacks he likes, but she did slip in a note telling him to have a fun day.

After school, Gabriel's mom picks him up for his piano lesson, giving him a Baggie of baby carrots for a snack and chiding him for a small hole that has appeared in his sock. Gabriel always dreads piano lessons—not only does his teacher smell like mothballs, but she always hums along while Gabriel plays. Gabriel's mom won't let him quit until he's been at it a year. She makes sure Gabriel says thank you to his teacher afterward. They stop by the dry cleaner and the grocery store on the way home.

Back at home, Gabriel is instructed to play inside since it rained during the day and the yard is muddy. He gets out his spacemen action figures, and his mom tells him to make sure to share with his little sister. When Dad comes home, Gabriel invites him to play Go Fish, but he doesn't have time. Soon, dinner is almost ready and Gabriel is asked to set the table. Sitting in his spot, he picks at the meal his dad has dished up for him, and is told that he has to finish his sweet potatoes or he won't be allowed to leave the table.

After dinner, Dad asks if Gabriel has any homework to do. He has one small assignment, so Dad works with him to make sure he finishes it. Then he asks Gabriel to play his piano piece for him— he likes to listen to Gabriel's progress—and soon after that, it's bathtime. Dad fills the tub for Gabriel and gets out a towel and washcloth. Gabriel splashes for about ten minutes before Dad scrubs behind his ears, reminding him it's time to finish washing up and hop out. Then Dad watches him brush his teeth, instructing him to get all the way to the back. He notices Gabriel's fingernails need trimming and helps him with that task. He lets him pick two stories ("but not the one about the monster again!") and then tells him to close his eyes and go to sleep. Gabriel asks for a glass of milk, and is given a small sip of water instead before drifting off.

WHAT A DAY. Now, here's what it would've looked like if Gabriel had been calling the shots:

Waking at 7:36, Gabriel hops out of bed. He bounces downstairs and finds Dad in the kitchen. Requesting his special blueberry pancakes for breakfast, Gabriel is soon pooling syrup on top of them. The school bus comes and goes as he's digging through the refrigerator for chocolate sauce to add. After breakfast, Gabriel plays with his spacemen action figures for a while before heading upstairs to put on his blue jeans with the hole in the knee and a gray sweatshirt with a truck on the front. He brushes neither his teeth nor his hair.

The morning is spent at the park, where Mom, who has skipped work today, pushes Gabriel on the swing for a grand total of one hour and seventeen minutes. For lunch, they enjoy a picnic on the living room floor, munching on grilled cheese sandwiches cut into the shape of monkeys and drinking strawberry milk out of bendy straws.

Then it's storytime with Dad, who has also called in sick to work, during which Dad acts out all the voices in a book about cars and another about frogs.

For a snack, Gabriel enjoys a large plate of cookies and some Jell-O. Then Mom and Dad both watch him ride circles on his bike in the driveway. He decides not to wear his helmet.

Once school would have normally let out, Gabriel invites his best friend over, and the two boys pull out all of Gabriel's toys and scatter them throughout the living room. He suggests pizza for dinner, and his parents readily comply, offering to go out for ice cream for dessert. The rest of the evening is spent playing Mousetrap with the whole family. Bedtime is delayed a good forty-five minutes and comes on the heels of eight stories, two songs and hot chocolate (with extra marshmallows).

DID you happen to notice the glaring disconnect between Gabriel and his parents? While it's likely that neither day plays out exactly the way we'd want our own households to run, the point is that the parents' priorities are not the child's priorities, and vice versa. In fact, at times they couldn't be more opposite.

As parents, we strive for order. We focus on productivity, goals and responsibilities. For example, our typical morning has us putting breakfast on the table for the whole family, making sure everyone is clean and dressed, and getting our kids off to school and ourselves off to work on time—all without turning the house into a disaster area. We constantly try to manage things, hold our lives together and move everyone and everything toward some goal as our basic mode of operation. Does that describe your life?

What's more, isn't it true that we could run our families just about perfectly—if we didn't have kids to throw a wrench into our well-laid plans? Let's face it—they could care less about our priorities. With a mode of operation that includes exploring, creating, experiencing new things and, most of all, having as much fun as possible, thoughts of clean underwear, straightened rooms and crayon-free walls are far from their minds. That's how they're wired, and it's how they learn. And since our priorities often conflict with our kids', tension enters the parent-child relationship.

A parent's priorities often overrule the child's with the myriad orders and directions we barrage them with every day. This is especially true in households where one or more parent has a Superiority or Controlling personality priority. But what's the big deal about that? Isn't it our job to direct our kids' lives?

What's the Big Deal About Power?

The big deal about power is that we, as parents, hold all of it, or try to. If asked, our kids would confirm this—they see us as the ones with all the power. We're the bedtime setters, the meal preparers, the allowance holders, the can-we-go-to-the-zoo-on-Saturday deciders and more. And most of the time we're good at it: we've been making important and not-so-important choices for our kids since before they were born.

It's no wonder, then, that power can be such an emotionally charged issue. We know that we're all hard-wired with a need for autonomy, free will and positive power. The control we have over everything, from what kind of juice we buy to whether or not the coolest new video game can come into our home, is enough to make any small person green with envy. It hardly seems fair, from a child's-eye view, and so they're determined to grasp some of that power for themselves whenever they get the chance.

But sometimes we really do have to get children to do what we want them to, don't we? After all, if Gabriel had his way, he'd stay home from school more often than not, and he'd be faced with a mouthful of cavities at his next dentist appointment—which probably wouldn't take place until he was getting his teeth whitened for job interviews.

Yes, you do need to wear the navigator's hat in your kids' lives as you help them gain wisdom and experience. And certainly, you should be the one making the big decisions and bringing a sense of order to your family.

The problem is, every single time you give your child a request, no matter how big or small, there's an opportunity for a power struggle as the child decides whether or not to jump up and obey you. Remember—your child's priorities are far different from your own. And from the terrible twos to the teenage terrors, the more we order, correct or direct our children, the more power struggles we can expect.

Looking back at Gabriel's parents' version of his day, can you see all the places where your child would have struggled for control? Although some of these issues, like going to school and going to bed, are non-negotiable, is there really a need for a potential power struggle every time we want our child to do something?

Is Power Worth Fighting For?

You'd think that as the people with all the power, parents would have power struggles figured out. We should "win" every one of them, right? But real life would suggest otherwise: They're among our most common challenges. Ironically, when we're engaged in a power struggle with even the smallest child, we're the ones feeling overpowered, possibly because our 3-year-old's unabashed writhing in the department store bothers us far more than it bothers her. There's hardly a household in the nation that doesn't wrestle internally for control.

And in each power struggle, the stakes are high. Take a typical dinnertime scenario:

ANNA's mom works hard to prepare nutritious meals for her family. And at times, her family works equally hard not to eat what she's cooked. Tonight is no exception—and Mom doesn't have her hopes up. There's broccoli on the table, and no amount of cheddar cheese piled on top can hide it.

"I'm not eating that," 7-year-old Anna warns her mom in advance.

"Just take some on your plate," Mom replies. After all, this is the first step toward eating some.

Anna dishes up two pieces of broccoli and then ignores them for the rest of the meal.

Mom, who has been monitoring the broccoli's status out of the corner of her eye, calmly mentions that Anna will have to eat a bite of it before she can leave the table.

"Yuck, I hate broccoli. I'm not eating it," Anna refuses.

"Oh yes you will, young lady. One bite. Now," Mom demands.

"No! It's disgusting!" Anna puts her foot down.

"It's good for you. You'll eat it." Mom's foot joins Anna's, and the brawl begins.

"You can't make me!" Anna reminds Mom.

"Yes I can, I'm your mother," Mom reminds Anna.

This continues for a good three minutes. Then Anna decides to solve the problem then and there: She throws the broccoli onto the floor. It's a big move, but a strategic one—if Mom can't make her eat it this time, she'll have to give in next time, too.

Now Mom's really mad. She scoops up the broccoli, washes it in the sink and puts it back on Anna's plate. If she can hold her ground this time, she tells herself, Anna will know who's boss and will back down more easily next time.

"Maybe if you could cook, it would taste okay!" snaps Anna angrily.

"Maybe if you would just give it a chance, you would learn to like it!" retorts Mom. She takes the broccoli and tries to shove it in Anna's mouth, but it soon becomes clear that won't work.

"No desserts for a week unless you try it!" Mom lays down the law.

Anna just ignores her: She's heard this before, and it wasn't too bad for the two whole days Mom ended up revoking her desserts.

Then Anna decides to put her fingers in her ears and scream loudly for a few minutes. Maybe a change in tactics will help. Irritated, and starting to realize that she can't win, Mom leaves the room. A few minutes later, so does Anna. Only the broccoli remains, shivering and limp on Anna's plate, as the rest of the family cleared out a while ago.

IN THIS battle for control, Anna appears to be the winner—after all, she didn't have to eat the broccoli. But is she, really? She had to resort to childish and somewhat degrading tactics to get her way. She learned nothing from the situation other than "Mom can't make me eat my broccoli" and remains resentful of Mom for the rest of the night.

For her part, by putting her foot down, Mom established competition between herself and her child. If she'd played her cards right, she probably could've "won," but may have resorted to threats, punishment or humiliation to do so. As it is, she engaged in a shouting match with a 7-year-old—which isn't exactly something to be proud of. She, too, leaves the situation feeling resentful. Do you think mom and daughter will be spending any Mind, Body & Soul Time together tonight?

What's more, there's the obvious fact that the whole household was passively involved in the fight. Whether a toddler is shrieking on the floor or a teenager is shouting and slamming doors, nobody likes to listen to a power struggle. It's grating on everyone's ears and nerves.

No matter who seems to come out ahead, power struggles are always a lose-lose situation. Pitting parent against child, they rob the child of a sense of significance and the chance to learn important decision-making skills. They catch everyone in their worst light. And with the right strategies, there's no reason to engage in one. There's a better way—a way to keep everyone's priorities in mind and foster a spirit of cooperation, all while teaching valuable lessons to your children. It begins with a change in how you think about power.

Empowering Children:
The Empowerment Paradigm

In chapter 1, we talked about parenting fifty years ago and parenting now. Fifty years ago, the authoritarian model of parenting dominated American households. The parents held the power—all of it—and repeatedly reminded the children of this fact in both words and actions. While kids often jumped to obey their parents under this system, and so it seemed quite functional at the time, we know that society has changed in ways that makes this model of leadership ineffective today.

With the concept of the democratic family, however, a new model of power distribution is emerging, even though the remnants of an authoritarian system are still present and followed. As you may remember, a democratic family isn't one in which everyone gets an equal vote—but everyone is equally welcome to share an opinion and equally obligated to share in the responsibilities. Each member of the household is empowered through this system to play an important role within the family and in the world. For this reason, I call it the Empowerment Paradigm. The tenets of this model are:

1. We *can't* control another person.
2. All we *can* control is ourselves and the environment.

And yes, tenet 1 applies to children as well as adults. It makes sense: Could Mom really *make* Anna eat her broccoli in the previous scenario? No—and she realized it. She tried commanding, threatening and even light physical force, but in the end, Anna held all the power. Nothing short of strapping Anna to a chair, prying open her mouth and shoving the bite down her throat was going to make Anna budge. So many aspects of our children's lives are out of our control, whether we like it or not. We may have the illusion of control, but our kids actually have the final say in most situations because most parents are, fortunately, unwilling to resort to Nazi-esque techniques to get their cooperation.

Family life shouldn't be a free-for-all, of course, but a household that operates with dignity and respect for all aligns surprisingly well with our parental ideals of raising healthy, happy kids who can shoulder their share of the responsibility, whether at home, at school or at work. This is the goal of the Empowerment Paradigm of parenting.

To achieve this goal, you'll need to relinquish what you can't control, and instead use what you can—yourself and your environment—to work toward the outcome you'd like to see with your kids. It's time to begin handing the reins over to your children. You'll need to empower them with the capabilities and the opportunities to think for themselves and act appropriately. Fortunately, relinquishing some power to your kids not only helps them build life skills, but it's also an effective strategy for reducing the power struggles that crop up during your day.

The upcoming tools, in this chapter and the next, will give you lots of strategies to use as you transfer positive power to your children, within your boundaries. Essentially, you'll be using your power to empower them. Doesn't that sound like an idea everyone in your house can get behind?

Take Time for Training

The Tool Explained

When you washed your newborn's first load of sweet little baby laundry, you probably didn't chuckle to yourself, "I hope I'm still doing this twenty years from now every time he brings his laundry home from college!" And yet, that's the situation so many parents find themselves in. We all want our kids to be capable and self-sufficient by the time they leave the house—if not much earlier—but getting them to that point can seem as daunting as crossing the ocean in a paddleboat.

Despite the fact that our kids may brutally fight every attempt we make to "civilize" them, they're spending their childhood undergoing a very slow, and very necessary, transition from dependence to independence. We see this most clearly in every power struggle we face—our kids might be fine depending on us when we're spooning ice cream into their bowls and playing Santa Claus, but they draw the line at age thirteen when we're telling them to put on something a little nicer than cutoffs and a T-shirt for their cousin's wedding. However, if we don't harness the natural forces at work, and miss out on opportunities to intentionally train our children in the practical skills they'll need in their adult lives, we're setting them up for a lifetime of relying on someone else to take care of them, whether that's us, a future spouse or some other person.

At the same time, have you ever realized that much of your child's training up to this point has come in the form of being told what *not* to do? It's easy for us to say, "Don't wear your shoes in the house," or "Don't leave your dirty dishes in the sink," but when we use a "don't" phrase, it only breeds confusion for our kids. Every time we say "don't," they have to double-process what we tell them in order to figure out what it is they're actually *supposed* to do. What's more, we leave the answer open to interpretation. Should they instead remove their shoes outside while balancing over the doorway and "air-conditioning the whole neighborhood"? Would it be better if they left their dirty dishes on the table, or deposited them into the garbage can? "Don't" phrases also have the unfortunate side effect of putting the actions we want our children to avoid directly into the forefront of their minds. So when you say, "Sit next to your sister but don't touch her," what do you think is going to happen next?

Beyond household responsibilities and good behavior, there are other life skills your kids need to learn. For instance, does anyone really know which fork to use at a nice dinner party when there are no fewer than three at their place? And wouldn't a lesson in how to escape the house in the event of a fire be helpful for all ages? Training throughout childhood should cover appropriate behaviors, household responsibilities and important information.

This tool will give you the information you need to begin the process of properly training your child in almost everything she'll need to know in the "real world." With training, "don't" phrases become unnecessary because our kids know what to *do*. This means less reminding on our part, and a greater sense of personal power on theirs. It'll take an investment of time and energy, but by empowering your kids through methodical training in everything from greeting an adult to balancing the checkbook, you can increase their feelings of significance, add to their capabilities and ensure that everyone contributes to the operation of your household.

Keep in mind that training is a process. By following the proper steps, and tailoring the information to your child's personality and the task you're training her in, you can foster success—and that boost of significance your child is craving. Here's how to get started.

First, choose an Age-Appropriate Task for your child from the list at the end of this tool (pages 118–120). Pick something that you think your child *could* do with proper training—not something she's already doing. Start with something she finds interesting. For instance, many young kids are fascinated with power tools and appliances. Your 4-year-old could use a handheld vacuum to clean up a mess, or your 12-year-old could push a lawn mower. Or maybe your 3-year-old is hosting tea parties with her dolls several times a day and would be open to learning table manners. Avoid "emotionally charged" areas like potty training—stick to something your child can learn with almost guaranteed success, so that she's excited about her accomplishment and open to more training in the future. Eventually, you can work toward training opportunities that will benefit the child and the parent, so the child will feel good about her contribution and will take some responsibility off your back.

Then, make a plan. Determine what you're going to teach and how you'll do it. Think about breaking the task into small steps so it will be easier for your child to master. Explain and demonstrate as you go; for instance, if you're training your child to do laundry, show him how you measure out detergent, teach him about different water levels and temperatures, and talk about instances when he may need to use a stain remover. Make sure he knows the "why" for every little thing you do. And finally, invite him to try it himself.

Get your child excited. Position the training in a positive light, and avoid accusing the child of having "slacked off" before, or anything that would put the child on the defensive. The training is a natural extension of growing up, and the new responsibility is something he needs to know because he's becoming independent.

Jump right in and start the training! You'll have fun and so will your child—even if you both make a few mistakes along the way.

When to Use It

- Whenever you feel that your child is ready to take on a new task or responsibility
- Whenever there's a behavior you'd like to teach

Why It Works

Training children in age-appropriate household tasks and the proper behavior in a variety of situations sets them up for short-term and long-term success. Each time your child manages a responsibility, he feels a huge boost in personal significance, power and independence. He experiences the positive effects of sharing in a household's responsibilities as well as its privileges, and can see how his contributions benefit the whole family.

Practically speaking, your child learns real-life skills while

Never do for a child what he can do for himself.
—Rudolf Dreikurs, M.D., author of *Children: The Challenge*

unburdening you. These are things we can't expect our kids to just pick up from watching us around the house. Not only would they lack the motivation, but even tasks like making toast can be intimidating to a child who's never done it on his own. When you take the time to deliberately train your child in a task or behavior, however, he'll learn everything he needs to know, not just the information he can glean out of the "don't" phrases we are apt to use. Although he may have his own methods for completing a task, he'll learn the pitfalls up front, and see at least one "right" way to do it to achieve the desired result. And with the correct training, he won't need you to nag or remind him about the task later.

Just as the jobs themselves don't always come naturally to kids, the ability to train doesn't always come naturally to us. Read on to learn how to get started, and how to make sure your training is effective.

Tips for Success

- When you choose a time to begin, make sure that:
  - □ Both you and the child are well-rested, well-fed and in the Adult Ego State so you'll be in the right frame of mind for sharing new information;
  - □ There will be as few distractions as possible during each training session;
  - □ You're at home and in a low-stress environment. (Don't try to train on table manners when you're at Grandma's house for Thanksgiving dinner!)
- Keep it light and make it fun. Be creative! Use role-play whenever possible—children love to act, and role-play can be a wonderful training tool. Invite dolls, stuffed animals and action

figures to participate. Switch roles and have your child "teach" you the right way to do it.

- Encourage any progress toward the goal, and look for improvement and effort. Avoid criticizing at all costs: When a child's learning something new, criticism can set the training process back for a long time. Remember, you've had decades of experience with the task that your child is just beginning to learn, and she doesn't have to do a job exactly how you would. If you need to, you can suggest, "One thing that works well for me is. . . . You could try that."

- Once your child has the task mastered at an age-appropriate level, add it to her list of family contributions. She'll be excited about a new "grown-up" way to contribute to your family. Yes, I'm realistic enough to know that the novelty of the new task will soon fade, so you'll learn how to make sure your child continues to do it in the next few chapters and tools.

Age-Appropriate Tasks*

2 TO 3 YEARS OLD

Wipe down kitchen chairs and stools with a damp sponge.

Carry in the newspaper or mail.

Pick up toys and clothes.

Wash tables and counters with a damp sponge.

Fold washcloths.

Wash vegetables, tear lettuce, stir.

Help set the table—napkins, silverware.

Feed the pets and refill water. (Be sure to provide training on just how much food and water to offer!)

---

*Adapted from Kathryn J. Kvols, *Redirecting Children's Behavior*.

Help clean own place at the table.

Help put groceries away at kid-friendly level.

Unload spoons and forks from dishwasher.

4 TO 5 YEARS OLD
Same as previous list, plus:

Make own bed—use a simple comforter.

Help fold towels and washcloths.

Clean own bathroom sink with wipes.

Water plants. (Provide training on how much water.)

Prepare simple breakfast/lunch and clean up.

Polish silver (wearing gloves).

Empty small trashcans around the house.

Sort white clothes from dark clothes for laundry.

Help with vacuuming, sweeping and dusting.

Transfer clothes from the washer to the dryer.

Dust mop the floor.

Use handheld vacuum for spills and messes.

6 TO 8 YEARS OLD
Same as previous list, plus:

Wash dishes; load and unload dishwasher.

Prepare simple dishes, such as salads and desserts.

Help change bedsheets and put dirty sheets in laundry.

Pack lunch for school.

Iron cloth napkins.

Fold simple laundry items and put them away.

Dust baseboards.

Vacuum and dust furniture.

Walk pets daily.

Pull weeds.

Get self up in the morning with an alarm clock.

Put groceries away.

9 TO 11 YEARS OLD

Same as previous list, plus:

Change lightbulbs and batteries, and do other household maintenance.

Fold all of own laundry and put it away.

Clean refrigerator, toilets and other more detailed household tasks.

Wash car and vacuum inside of car.

Plant flowers and garden items at change of season.

Assist younger siblings with homework and reading.

Bathe and groom pets.

Gather trash, take it out, and do other weekly trash duties.

Organize closet and drawers monthly.

12 TO 14 YEARS OLD

Same as previous list, plus:

Change bedsheets independently.

Do laundry start to finish.

Wash indoor windows and lower outdoor windows.

Mow lawn, rake leaves, spread mulch.

Help with administrative tasks in parents' business.

Prepare family meal one day a week using a simple menu.

Manage family recycling efforts.

Babysit siblings for short periods with adult nearby.

Have total responsibility for family pets.

Clean shower and tub.

Choices

The Tool Explained

All kids are hard-wired with a need for power—and if we don't provide them with power in positive ways, they'll resort to negative means to get it. One of the most effective ways to transfer positive power to your kids is to allow them opportunities, little by little, to practice making decisions. At the same time, you can prevent power struggles, put an end to misbehaviors and foster cooperation—all by giving your children choices in a variety of situations.

Choices are best used throughout the day either to offer opportunities for your child to gain positive power, or to ward off power struggles (or both). Most often, you should anticipate the choice. For instance, if your child resists brushing his teeth, you can let him choose between the alligator toothbrush or the football toothbrush. Either way, he'll be brushing his teeth, but when he's focused on the choice of toothbrush, he may not even remember to fight about it. The potential power struggle is avoided, your child has benefited from making his own decision and your goal is accomplished. You can also use choices as you see a power struggle brewing—if your child refuses to take the dog out, you can invite her to choose between playing with Buddy in the yard, or walking him around the block.

And while it's fine to offer choices as part of your response to your child's negative behavior, when you proactively offer choices to your kids throughout the day, you'll create a spirit of cooperation and instill in them the all-important sense of personal power. As a result, your children will be less likely to misbehave in the first place and you'll see an overall decrease in power struggles in your house.

When to Use It

- Regularly throughout the day
- In any situation when you often face a power struggle, or to defuse an imminent struggle
- Whenever you would normally choose something for your kids, as long as the options fit within your boundaries—for example, when picking the flavor of yogurt at the grocery store
- Only in matters when there's actually a choice (e.g., bedtime isn't a choice, but the bedtime story is)
- When you've noticed an overall increase in power-seeking misbehavior, as a way to foster a general sense of cooperation

Why It Works

Choices are a wonderful tool for providing a sense of positive power to your kids. They lead to a heightened feeling of significance and give children a sense of dominion over their own lives. And as kids will find a way to get power somehow, we can stop and prevent quite a few negative behaviors by giving it to them up front.

A proactive choice timed well provides a boost of positive power at the moment when a child would normally feel as if she's lost it. When instead of telling your child to get into the bathtub you offer her a simple choice in the color of washcloth to use, you allow her to continue with the task at hand without feeling overpowered. Your daughter gains a sense of significance even as she's demonstrating the proper behavior. Instead of welcoming a power struggle, you've invited cooperation.

What's more, choices empower your kids on your own terms. You'd certainly never give the choice "Would you like green beans for lunch, or cookies?" But you could offer to cut a peanut-butter sandwich into either a fish or a frog using cookie cutters. And by providing options that you can live with, you remove some of your own stress from the situation. After all, does it really matter to you whether your son works off steam by hitting a pillow or stomping like a dinosaur, as long as he's not taking it out on his older brother?

And we shouldn't gloss over the power of distraction that choices can provide. Any decision temporarily takes the focus off the behavior that you either want to enforce (like handwashing before dinner) or put a stop to (such as trying to climb shelves). When your child has a couple of options to consider, putting up a struggle might not even cross her mind.

Finally, by providing your kids with choices and a sense of personal power throughout the day, they continually receive the doses of significance they crave. This means they won't need to resort to other, more negative means to get it. As you implement this tool, you should see negative power-seeking behaviors decrease, so that even when you can't offer a choice you'll be less likely to encounter resistance. What's more, your kids will benefit from making real decisions and experiencing small amounts of power for themselves.

Tips for Success
- Start with a list. Until you're used to offering choices regularly, you can jot down a quick list of your daily activities and the options you can offer for each one.
- Use creative thinking to turn almost any task or behavior into

a choice. Young kids, especially, will be eager to choose between characters, colors, shapes and more. Other options include the order two tasks are done in, methods for accomplishing a goal or how much help to receive from a parent.

- Don't go overboard. Not everything has to be a choice (after all, that's not very realistic). And there's no reason to offer unlimited choices—two are usually enough.

Below are some ideas to get you started offering choices.

HOMEWORK

Would you like to do your homework before or after snack?

Would you rather do your homework in the kitchen or in your bedroom?

BATHTIME

Should we use the blue or the yellow towel?

Would you like your bath toys in the water or sitting on the side of the tub?

Should I soap you or should you soap yourself?

BRUSHING TEETH

Which toothpaste/toothbrush do you want to use?

Who should brush your teeth first: you or Daddy?

GETTING OUT THE DOOR

Do you want to put on your shoes first, or your jacket?

Would you rather look at a book in the car or listen to your CD?

Should we go to the post office first, or stop by the mall?

BEDTIME

Would you like your bunny or your bear?

Do you prefer your nightgown or your footy pajamas?

Would you like me to read to you, or would you rather read on your own?

HOUSEHOLD HELP

Would you rather make the salad or set the table?

Do you prefer to unload the top or bottom of the dishwasher?

Would you rather fold and put away the darks or the whites?

A Better Day for Everyone

Let's take a final look at Gabriel's day. Here's how it might have played out if his parents had used some empowering strategies.

EVERY MORNING at seven, 6-year-old Gabriel bounces out of bed to the tunes on his favorite CD that plays in his alarm clock. He pulls on a blue sweatshirt and jeans from the "school clothes" section of his closet, and then combs his hair and washes his face before heading downstairs for breakfast. Gabriel picks out his breakfast cereal and sits down to eat. Mom offers Gabriel his choice of a pear or a banana in his lunchbox and then notes that it's looking pretty dark and cloudy outside. "Do you need anything else for school?" she asks. Gabriel thinks a moment, and then decides to grab an umbrella.

When Gabriel asks if he can invite a friend home from school, Mom reminds him about his piano lesson scheduled for that afternoon, but gives him the choice of either inviting the friend the next day, or on Saturday morning. After all, he's free all day Saturday—when he started piano lessons (which he doesn't enjoy, but is trying for a year), he decided that he'd rather take them after school than on Saturday mornings. Gabriel plans to ask his friend over Saturday, and then goes back upstairs to brush his teeth and gather his things. As he heads out the door for school, Mom hands him his lunch bag and mentions that she knows bologna isn't his favorite, but at the grocery store that afternoon they can choose what he'd like in his sandwiches for the next few days. She's left a note in the bag for him mentioning that she'd love to either go to the park with him that weekend or have a movie night, and he can decide (she's even drawn a little check box beside each choice).

After school, Gabriel's mom picks him up for his piano lesson, offering him either baby carrots or apple slices for a snack. She notices a small hole in his pants and asks, sympathetically, if he hurt himself. When Gabriel says he just caught the pant leg on the slide, she suggests that he help her find the right color of thread so she can patch it up. Gabriel dreads piano lessons—not only does his teacher smell like mothballs, but she always hums along while Gabriel plays. But he knows he can pick something new to try once he's taken piano for a year. Gabriel remembers to say thank you— he's practiced at home through role-playing with Dad and Buzz Lightyear. On the way back to the house, they stop by the dry cleaner and the grocery store, where Gabriel decides he'd like ham-and-cheese sandwiches in his lunch.

Back at home, the yard is muddy from rain, so Gabriel is given the choice to play in the living room, where he'll have to share toys with his sister, or in his room, where she's not allowed unless invited. He gets out his spacemen action figures and heads for the living room—there's more space and his sister doesn't usually want to play with them. When Dad comes home, he asks Gabriel to help him make the salad for dinner. They chat about Gabriel's day as he tears lettuce, and Dad gives him a quick lesson on peeling and cutting cucumbers. At dinner, Gabriel chooses to eat salad instead of the sweet potatoes.

After dinner, Dad asks if Gabriel has any homework to do. He has one small assignment, and Dad gives him his choice of doing it in his room or at the kitchen table. He picks the table, so Dad sits next to him and checks his e-mail on his laptop, letting Gabriel know, "I have confidence that you know what you're doing, but I'm here if you'd like to run anything by me." With the remaining time before bathtime, Dad says he'd love to hear Gabriel's piano piece if he'd be willing to play it. Gabriel agrees—but just one song, one time. Then he plays with his spacemen for a few more minutes, and it's time for his bath. Dad fills the tub while Gabriel chooses a towel and washcloth. Gabriel then decides he'd rather wash up quickly than play an extra few minutes—that way, as Dad noted, they'll have time for two stories at bedtime. After Gabriel's brushed and flossed his teeth, he gets some training from Dad in trimming his fingernails. Gabriel does one hand while Dad does the other. Gabriel sets his alarm for the next day. Then Dad reads two stories—with all the appropriate voices—and Gabriel soon drifts off to sleep.

As you can see, Gabriel's day was filled with positive power. Even though he completed the same tasks, they left him feeling empowered as he made good choices for himself and learned about appropriate behavior. And that's what we want for our kids, too.

Tools like offering choices and taking time for training are excellent ways to empower your children and continue to foster positive behavior in your household. But the struggle for power is only part of the story. In the next chapter, we'll talk about the battle for control—and how with the proper tools, there really doesn't need to be a battle at all.

USING WHAT YOU CAN
CONTROL TO MANAGE
WHAT YOU CAN'T

The Empowerment Paradigm, which we covered in the previous chapter, tells us that while we can't control another person, we can control ourselves and our environment. Now that you've begun to empower your kids with training and choices, it's time to dig into the concept of control with four new tools that you'll soon come to rely on.

These tools represent four different strategies for controlling a situation. All are based on managing your reactions and the environment around you—the two things that are firmly within your power. They offer your children a sense of positive power in situations when they'd normally try to engage you in a power struggle.

But first, you need to make sure you're committed to letting go of the illusion of control you may have if you see yourself as solely an authority figure over your child. Remember, you can't force a child to eat broccoli, say "please" and "thank you" or go to sleep, short of resorting to Nazi-esque techniques. Once you understand and accept this fact, you can let go of power struggles and instead focus on the things you can control to influence positive actions in your child. Trust me, you'll be much happier this way, and your children will be, too.

TOOLBOX SOLUTION #6

Decide What *You* Will Do

The Tool Explained

As parents, we're now well aware—both in theory and in practice—that we can't control our children's actions. But we can control our own. This tool gives you the power to decide what action *you* will take in response to your kids' misbehaviors so that your kids learn from their mistakes and you don't get stuck solving problems that aren't yours.

There are two things at stake in this tool. The first is your child's misbehavior. For example, you can't force your children to make sure all of their dirty clothes are in their hampers when you're ready to launder them. But what you *can* do is decide how you will handle the laundry situation in your house. For example, inform the family that laundry day is Tuesday, and you will only wash clothes that are in laundry hampers. Any clothes that aren't in the hamper will have to wait until the next laundry day—or they can be washed by their owner. You can bet that the first time Daniel is forced to wear a jersey that's neither clean nor pleasant-smelling for practice, he'll make a special effort to remember his laundry next Tuesday.

The second thing at stake is your own sanity. In the laundry example, for instance, Mom saves herself the trouble of nagging and reminding her kids to use their hampers throughout the week, tracking down dirty clothes on laundry day and then running an extra minuscule load or two as kids find the jeans they *have* to wear to school the next day or the uniform that needs to be sparkling clean for marching band—but spent the night in the car instead of the hamper.

Beyond household tasks, this tool can address quite a few of those annoying negative behaviors that tend to come up. For instance, if your child constantly whines, you can simply choose not to listen. Or if your toddler is experimenting with screeching, you can leave the room (and take away any attention your toddler was receiving from you).

When to Use It

- When you want to reduce repeated misbehaviors
- When you constantly find yourself nagging about the same thing
- When you end up doing things for your kids they should be doing for themselves

Why It Works

The most explosive power struggles happen when we're trying to control someone else. This tool works because it's based on the premise that you *can't* control someone else, so you instead need to control your reaction. Once you determine what you're willing to do, it ends the battle for power: You're no longer trying to force your child do something he doesn't want to do, and you're making the situation work for you no matter what your child does.

The Decide What *You* Will Do tool puts responsibility squarely on your kids' shoulders, whether you're trying to encourage a positive action or discourage a negative one. And if your child is unwilling to take on the responsibility, he loses out on a privilege. For instance, you can decide that as long as lunchboxes are empty, clean and on their appropriate shelf in the pantry, you will fill them every morning. However, if lunchboxes are not in their places, or contain yesterday's leftovers, lunch will not be packed in them and the owners will be responsible for packing their own lunches. Your child will quickly learn that the privilege of having lunch packed for him comes with the responsibility of making sure his lunchbox is ready to go.

This tool also commands respect—your kids learn that you're not a doormat, nor are you a personal maid or short-order cook. It sets fair and reasonable boundaries that everyone can live with, and is empowering for everyone involved. It works great for Pleasers and Comforters (remember your personality priority?) because it gives these types a way to avoid taking on responsibility that should belong to their children. And it helps Controllers and Superiors keep from nagging endlessly until a task is completed.

Tips for Success
- Be clear when you're informing your child what you will (or will not) do in a specific situation. Make sure she understands so that she can take on the responsibility, or learn from it if she chooses not to.

- Have the What *You* Will Do discussion at a calm time, and not in the heat of the moment. If you speak it in anger, you'll only create a power struggle.
- Be consistent. Your kids will test you several times before they're convinced you're serious.
- Follow through. This tool won't work unless you do what you say you'll do. Hold firm, or you'll lose ground.

TOOLBOX SOLUTION #7

Control the Environment

The Tool Explained

Aside from controlling our own responses to our kids, we can also control the environment within our house to encourage the behaviors we want to see and discourage the ones we don't. You can use the Control the Environment tool two different ways, whether you're working to empower your kids in everyday tasks or to defuse power struggles.

This tool is especially helpful for developing independence in your children by making your house kid-friendly. You've probably done this in the past with an eye for safety by baby-proofing and toddler-proofing stairs, outlets, shelves and more. As kids grow older, similar types of changes can facilitate a 5-year-old making herself a sandwich, a 9-year-old wrapping presents or a 13-year-old blending a healthy smoothie for herself rather than just grabbing a bag of chips. To get started, you can arrange pantries, refrigerators, closets and other areas to facilitate small hands and short people fixing their own bowl of cereal or hanging up their own clothes. Smaller containers for milk, juice and healthy snacks can help your child help himself. Closet rods installed at kid height give kids the power to select their own clothing for school, while adult-height rods allow you to keep out-of-season clothing out of reach. Kids also appreciate special bins for toys, craft supplies, sports equipment and more, to help keep things organized. For older children and teenagers, simply making sure supplies for mailing letters, cleaning a wound or pumping up bicycle tires are readily available and easy to find might be enough. A small investment in time and money to strategically arrange your environment will pay off as your children naturally shoulder more responsibility—or at least don't have a good excuse not to.

Another great use for this tool is to eliminate negative behaviors. Lots of everyday power struggles can be avoided simply by keeping triggers out of sight and out of mind. For instance, if your children constantly beg you for sweets, you can simply quit buying them and keep them out of your house. If your kids always whine for more books at bedtime, store them out of the bedroom and only bring a predetermined number in for the nighttime routine. And your kids can't insist on wearing shorts to go play in the snow if they're packed away in the attic until spring.

What about your house? Take a look around, and see if you can make some simple changes that will either help your kids gain some independence or avoid volatile situations. Even a few small adjustments can make a big difference, and the whole family will be happier for it.

When to Use It

- When you want to encourage independence in a specific task
- When you want to correct a repeated misbehavior

- This weekend! A careful look around your house, and possibly a trip to the store, can jump-start your use of this tool. One Saturday afternoon's worth of work could go a long way as your kids take on more responsibility.

Why It Works

Kids naturally respond to their environment—we all do. Consider the fish tank at the dentist's office that soothes and distracts your children as they wait for their appointment, or the colorful lights and upbeat music at the pizza place your family loves. Businesses know that the environment sets a tone and promotes any number of calculated behaviors, from patient waiting to funky fun. In the same way, controlling your kids' surroundings can go a long way in influencing their actions and moving them toward more positive ones.

A well-organized house that's set up to run efficiently, even for the littlest hands, will naturally invite kids to participate in the responsibilities of taking care of themselves and the house. For one, they won't have to guess where to put away their toys if they have bins labeled with words or pictures to help them figure it out. And many children enjoy lending a hand in the kitchen, but so often we're the ones who won't let them for fear they'll spill an entire gallon of milk all over the kitchen floor.

We can all probably relate to the daily dilemma of getting our kids dressed in the morning. We make sure their closets are stocked full of clothes appropriate for any weather or occasion. And then little Emma appears in a red plaid skirt, purple knee socks, orange jellies and a green tank top with a blueberry stain on it for school picture day in kindergarten (or any other day, for that matter), and we cringe at our inner need to ask her to go change. Or maybe we select an outfit for each young child in our household the night before—but then we're still left with the struggle of convincing them to actually wear it. The best option to build a sense of significance is certainly to let kids pick out their own clothes, whether they go together or not. But there are ways to control the environment so that your internal drive to make sure your kids' clothes match is met. Try hanging a rack at your child's height, and group outfits on the same hanger. Even a 2-year-old can choose her own outfit this way—and what a wonderful boost of personal power!

The best part about controlling the environment so that your kids can adopt more independence is that they'll really feel a sense of dominion over their own lives. So often, kids feel that parents call all the shots. But with an environment that welcomes their participation, children get to have a lot more say. Simply being able to fix a snack without having to ask Mom for help can be very empowering.

As for the repeated negative behaviors we'd like to avoid, we can make huge strides in reducing these actions by removing or replacing the objects that trigger them. Controlling the environment for ourselves might involve getting a friend to hide all our chocolate, or cutting up credit cards. For your kids, it might mean installing software that limits their screen time or the websites they visit, buying only snack-size packs of chips and other goodies, or putting away toys that always seem to cause frustration. Removing these things from your children's environment will compel them to find better options for snacktime, their free time and more.

While you still can't control your kids, you can foster greater cooperation by managing their environment. It might take some trial and error to get your house into shape, but it'll be well worth the effort in the long run.

Tips for Success

- While you may be tempted to throw your child's video games into the trash just to end the badgering about getting extra video game time, start with a less drastic approach—for instance, store all the games in a box on the closet shelf until all homework is done. If that doesn't solve the problem, pack the game system away for a few months until your child is older and has developed the maturity to turn the system off when gaming time is up. The same applies for other situations—start with something less drastic, and then increase your control over the environment if you need to.

- Keep watch for things you're doing for your child that she could do herself. Small children, especially, develop new skills at a rapid pace, so you might find that while last month your child couldn't hold a small pitcher steady enough to pour juice, this month she probably could.

- Follow through. If you invest in child-sized containers or organizer bins, expect your kids to use them. And if you pack away a foam baseball bat that's gotten misused against a sibling too many times, keep it packed away until you decide your child can handle it again—not when she's begging to play with it.

When-Then

The Tool Explained

Parents tell me that When-Then works like magic for getting kids to cooperate without a battle, even kids who are considered strong-willed. It can be used for kids of all ages, and in almost any situation—even in the throes of a power struggle—and is empowering for parents and children.

The main concept behind When-Then is to delay or deny a normally occurring privilege until a task is done. When used effectively, it cuts out all of the "But I don't want to!" or "It's not fair!" after you've asked your youngest to empty the dishwasher, and completely shuts down any chance at a power struggle. It's as simple as this:

> Dad: *Easton, it's almost time for dinner, will you please empty the dishwasher?*
> Easton: *I'm busy, get Caroline to do it!*
> Dad: *When you empty the dishwasher, then you can join us for dinner.*
> Dad calmly walks away.

Easton is left with a decision—empty the dishwasher or he won't be able to eat supper. You can bet which one he'll choose. With no one left to whine to, and a clear understanding of what needs to happen, he has every reason to comply.

To deliver your own When-Then, follow this formula:

1. Develop the "when." This is the task you ask your child to do (wash up for dinner, rake the leaves in the yard, walk the dog, etc.), anticipating some version of a "no" answer.

2. Develop the "then." Think of a normally occurring privilege you can delay or deny your child until the task is complete. Make sure it's timely in relation to the task. For instance, the dishwasher needs to be emptied soon—so revoking a special trip to the bowling alley planned for tomorrow probably won't solve the problem. However, dinner is in thirty minutes, so that becomes the perfect "then."

3. In your Calm Voice, state the When-Then to your child, emphasizing the "when" and the "then." "When you . . . , then you can . . . ." Say it only once, and make sure you're clear.

4. Disengage or walk away. This is absolutely necessary for the When-Then to work. Busy yourself with something else so you won't be tempted to respond if your child tries to argue.

5. Be consistent in how you structure your When-Thens. Your kids will come to learn that if you start a sentence with "when," you mean business—and there's no sense in arguing.

6. Smile in amazement as your child first hesitates, and then jumps to do what you've asked!

When to Use It

- When you want your child to take action and do something he doesn't want to do.
- For kids older than 2½. Children need to have good verbal skills and an understanding of cause and effect, or else the tool won't work. For kids younger than this, offering Choices (tool #5) is an effective strategy.

Why It Works

When-Then acts as a highly potent tool to defuse power struggles because it gives your child positive power, and still accomplishes your goal. It's simply another way to control the environment—you're not controlling your child, but you are adjusting the order of events.

This isn't to say your kids will love this tool—in fact, you might meet with sighs and eye rolls as you begin using it more often. But with every When-Then, your child gains the control to decide when she will be able to access a normally occurring privilege. The power is in her hands. And as if by magic, every time you use it—and walk away afterward—a power struggle that normally could have escalated into a shouting match will simply fade away. Your children can't argue if there's no one to argue with and if they have a perfectly acceptable way to get what they want.

By leaving the scene of the situation (even if you just turn away to do a different task), you also empower your kids to follow through with their part of the When-Then and save face. Your body language will tell them you're not planning to negotiate, but that you have complete confidence in their capabilities to complete the job.

Parents often wonder whether the "then" acts as a reward. The reason it's not a reward is because you're allowing (or denying) your child a *normally occurring* privilege. This is something they'd be able to have or do anyway, not a special treat.

Tips for Success

- Make sure the "then" is something your child cares about. If he doesn't care about dinner, then his TV/video time may be a better "then" option.

- Remain in the Parent Ego State and use your Calm Voice when delivering the When-Then. It helps to plaster a smile on your face, even if it's fake!

- Always structure your When-Then the same way so that your kids know what's coming. They'll be less likely to try to argue if you're consistent with your words and follow through.

- It's "when," not "if." Not only does "if" make the statement feel like a bribe, it also implies you don't have confidence that your child will get the job done.

- Adopt an attitude of indifference. If your kids sense that you're stressed about the situation, it'll only induce them to add fuel to it.

- Don't offer reminders—they only invite more whining. After you've spoken your When-Then clearly one time, remove yourself from the conversation.

- Completely ignore any back talk or disrespectful comments your kids make as you deliver the When-Then. Your children have a right to gripe, and you have a right not to pay any attention. As you begin to use When-Thens consistently, the griping will quickly subside—your kids will realize there's no point.

- Set a deadline, if one is appropriate, to make sure your kids are clear about when they need to have a task completed. For instance, "When you finish walking the dog, then you can join us for dinner. Remember, the kitchen closes at six-thirty." Or,

"When your teeth are brushed and flossed, then we'll read stories until lights-out at eight."

- If your kids haven't completed the task you've assigned them in a reasonable amount of time, deny them the privilege (the "then" part of the When-Then). If you give them a second chance, they'll learn that you're willing to negotiate. That means that if Alexander shows up at 6:50 wondering where his supper is, you need to say, "Oh gosh, the kitchen is already closed for the evening but I'm confident you'll be able to get everything done before dinner tomorrow night." Make sure you follow through by refusing any requests for snacks before bedtime.
- If there's no applicable normally occurring privilege you can delay or deny, choose a different strategy. Avoid creating a privilege simply to use a When-Then, as this would become a reward.

Make When-Then Routines the Boss

The Tool Explained

You've heard it before: Set a routine for your kids. If you think your current routines could use a tune-up, and especially if you're having trouble getting your kids ready to go in the morning or sending them to bed, I strongly encourage you to give When-Then Routines a shot. I call my version the When-Then Routine because it follows the same format as the When-Then in tool #8. *When* your kids complete the items in the routine, *then* they get to enjoy a normally occurring privilege. Follow a routine consistently, and soon it'll have your house running much more smoothly—routines really work!

When-Then Routines are a method of controlling your children's environment, and they'll cut back substantially on the nagging and reminding you may find yourself doing on a daily basis. They can be particularly helpful in the morning, after school, at bedtime and during other potentially volatile times of the day.

When you establish a routine, it's key to make sure the last thing on the list is the most desirable action. For instance, your kids' morning routine could include non-negotiables like making their beds, getting dressed, washing up and putting backpacks and lunchboxes by the door. Finally, once everything else is done, they can come to the table for breakfast. This assumes that your kids are eager to eat, so if they're not, you can allow morning playtime, or ten minutes of TV time within your routine, once everything else is completed and before it's time to leave for school. Both of these are normally occurring privileges for a child ready ahead of schedule, and not special rewards.

Routines work best when you set them up as a When-Then situation (see tool #8). So *when* all your kids' tasks are finished in the morning, *then* they are welcome to eat breakfast in the time remaining before the bus leaves. Yes, your kids may go to school hungry if they don't get everything done—but rest assured this will happen only once.

To develop this type of routine, begin by writing a list of the non-negotiables, or the things that must be done. This is your "when." Then create a desirable action to happen as the last thing— your "then"—and place a deadline (the school bus arriving, or bedtime) if appropriate. Make sure you present the routine to your kids in this format.

I encourage you to solicit your older kids' input into their routine. A 13-year-old can decide for herself whether she wants to shower in the morning or in the evening, for instance, and a 10-year-old can choose in which order to do homework and family contributions. By asking your kids' preferences, you also get buy-in for the routine, and your kids are less likely to feel overpowered by their parents.

Many parents wonder if rewards come into play as the last item in the routine, but as we discussed in the When-Then tool, they don't. The desirable action should be something that would happen anyway, not a special treat.

To begin using the routine, make sure you present it to your kids at a neutral time, and review it to make sure everyone understands what's expected. Then, post it (if necessary) in a logical location—for instance, in the kitchen if it's a morning routine that ends with breakfast. If your 8-year-old appears the next morning in his pajamas asking for scrambled eggs, you can simply say with a smile, "Good to see you! *When* you are dressed and have finished your routine, *then* you can have breakfast." Then disengage or walk away—your child won't be able to negotiate or argue if you refuse to respond.

Of course, you don't need a routine for everything that happens during the day—kids need plenty of unstructured time, too. However, you can cut back on power struggles significantly when you make routines the boss at the times when you'd rather not be.

When to Use It

- Morning, after school, bathtime, bedtime, mealtimes and/or other difficult, yet fairly predictable, times of the day
- Whenever your kids seem to push back and negotiate over everyday tasks
- Summertime. A special routine for school-free months can help everyone make the best use of their time off and ensure that family contributions get done without nagging and reminding from Mom and Dad.

Why It Works

When-Then Routines work because they're a win-win situation for parents and kids, and the benefits are numerous. Not only do they cut down on power struggles and negotiations, they set the stage for an orderly home.

It's long been accepted that children of all ages thrive on the predictability of a routine. Kids and adolescents are hard-wired with a need for order, and knowing what happens next—even if they don't particularly like it   provides a feeling of security. And when you structure a routine so that the last item on the list is something enjoyable, children feel a sense of control and accomplishment in reaching that desirable goal.

Routines are a parent's best friend when it comes to reducing power struggles. When there's a logical, orderly procession of events that's been established, the pressure is lifted from the parents—they're no longer the "bad guy." Take bedtime, for instance. If bedtime on Monday night is 7:30, and on Tuesday it's 8:05, and by the weekend it's 9:30, there's obviously no set bedtime—and kids know it. That means it's up for negotiation every single evening.

Why should your children go to bed at 7:30 if last night they got to stay up two hours later? With a routine, though, bedtime is the "law" in your household. Kids know not to argue or negotiate, because there will be no payoff—bedtime won't change no matter what they say. The routine becomes the boss so you don't have to.

This works in other matters, too. Once kids understand that homework and piano practice have to be completed before they can call their friends, they'll quit badgering you about it. Very soon, they'll understand that the power to access their privilege is in their own hands—so the less they argue, the faster they'll be able to enjoy themselves.

Tips for Success

- Every day, your kids should have some family contributions: There's no free ride in your house and everyone has to contribute for the family to function. You can incorporate family contributions into their routines if that helps them get completed. On weekends, it's reasonable for your kids to have a few extra family contributions.
- Keep bedtimes consistent every night of the week. Most kids get far less sleep than they need, and one of the reasons is a shifting bedtime, particularly on weekends. Children's bodies don't recognize weekends, so they usually wake up at the same time each morning no matter when they've gone to sleep the night before. They need the same amount of sleep each night, so letting them stay up late will only make for overtired kids on Monday morning.
- When you use a bedtime routine with younger kids who don't quite have a concept of time yet, use a timer. You can put an end to dawdling if you let them know that bedtime is when the

timer goes off—with or without stories. If they finish soon enough (allow plenty of time), they'll be able to enjoy story-time. If they dawdle, there won't be enough time for a retelling of the Three Little Pigs. Don't worry, they'll catch on quickly!

- Create a different routine for the summer, or whenever your kids are out of school for a long period of time. Add a few family contributions to be completed each day, for instance, before kids can play with their friends or enjoy technology time.

- Your summer routine may shift bedtime a bit later, but bedtime should still be consistent every day of the week.

- Use a simple checklist on a clipboard for young kids to help them keep track of the things they need to do to complete their routine, with pictures if your child can't read yet. Any list with more than a couple of items might be too much for a child to commit to memory. This isn't the same as a sticker chart, which uses stickers as rewards (and so should be avoided).

- Smile! There's no need to get worked up with enforcing a routine. Use your Calm Voice, and let the routine shoulder the hard work. That's what it's for.

- Be consistent, and follow through. Ignore any attempts to negotiate, and soon your kids won't bother.

Tools #6 through #9, as well as the tools in previous chapters, will help you navigate or completely avoid almost any power struggle you face by relinquishing power over what you can't control (your child) and strategically controlling what you can (yourself and your environment). As you put these tools to good use, you'll likely notice a reduction in your battles for power with your kids. After all, you're providing them with plenty of the positive power they need—on your terms.

THE POSITIVE SIDE
OF MISBEHAVIOR

Learning Life's Lessons

It would seem that Bella is just about the most forgetful girl in her third-grade class. She's kind to her peers, she pays attention and her work is above average, and yet several times a week Bella's mom pops her head into the classroom with a forgotten lunch, rain boots, library books, a permission slip, an interesting seashell for show-and-tell, mittens—even Bella's shoes one time when she accidentally made it all the way to school without changing out of her pink bunny slippers.

It's not that Bella's parents haven't tried. Every evening, they remind her to gather her things for school the next day. Her mom packs a lunch for her every morning and leaves it by the door, along with anything else she can think of that her daughter might need. But as Bella runs out of the house to the school bus, she invariably forgets to grab her sheet music for her after-school violin lesson, or her tennis shoes for gym class.

And then, after getting an apologetic and somewhat frantic phone call from Bella asking if she can drop off her pond diorama project or her math homework, Bella's mom sighs and hops in the car for the ten-minute drive to school. Bella is always properly grateful and promises to "never forget this again!" but Bella's mom knows by now that within a couple of days, she'll be coming back to Bella's rescue.

SOME KIDS are merely forgetful. Others demonstrate an inner resolve not to do what we ask, and still others simply seem not to care enough to be responsible or behave appropriately. But the fact of the matter is that misbehavior comes in all forms—and the obligation to address it falls squarely on our shoulders.

Bella's mom, who probably didn't mind doing a quick run to school at first, may now feel like her daughter will never grow out of her forgetfulness. And she's probably right: An expression in parenting education circles notes, "A child who always forgets has a parent who always remembers."

So what do we do? When a particularly big challenge presents itself, how do we manage?

When faced with even as little an obstacle as "I don't want to put my shoes on to go to the grocery store," many parents' natural instinct is to resort to punishment. But we know from chapter 1 that punishment isn't effective in accomplishing anything good, such as empowering our children and training them in appropriate behavior. Instead, it gives rise to anger, resentment, fear and lying to avoid future punishment. Fortunately, there are ways to address tough misbehaviors without resorting to such punitive means. You might be surprised to see that in some instances, your best resort is to do nothing at all.

When you're met with a challenging behavior, whether your 11-year-old refuses to wear anything heavier than a T-shirt during the coldest winter on record, or your 3-year-old has turned the teeth-brushing battle into an all-out war, your first response should be to make sure you're using all of the tools we've introduced up until this point. While the three tools in this chapter can be extremely powerful, they won't be effective unless there's a solid foundation of belonging and significance developed through Mind, Body & Soul Time, Take Time for Training, Choices and the rest. These initial tools empower your children, and should already be at work in reducing the misbehaviors in your home before you implement the tools described below. For example, Bella's mom could benefit from implementing a When-Then Routine that includes a checklist every morning to give Bella a chance to slow down and really think about what she needs for school.

However, sometimes you need something more, and that's where consequences come in. Consequences are for the times when Isaac absolutely won't, no question about it, brush his teeth—whether his toothbrush is orange or green, whether it's part of his routine or not. Or for when Maggie simply can't be convinced to put on a jacket (let alone a hat and gloves) to walk to school in a blizzard, regardless of your When-Then.

Operating from the basic theory of cause and effect (which your child will likely understand by the age of 2½), consequences allow *life* to be the teacher as you train for good behavior in the future. Empowering for adults and children alike, they essentially provide kids a choice: Demonstrate proper behavior (brushing your teeth, wearing a coat), or you're welcome to feel the real, negative effects of your poor choice.

"That sounds like punishment!" most parents are quick to inform me. But consequences are very different from punishment, in that they don't harm your child physically or emotionally, they focus on future behavior instead of past behavior and they are revealed in advance to your children so there will be no surprises (otherwise, they feel like punishment to your kids). What's more, they really make sense to kids since they directly address the misbehavior. If events simply play out, consequences allow kids to learn from their mistakes. No, your children won't enjoy the consequences of their negative actions—but they'll be quick to adopt better behavior next time, and more quickly and agreeably than on the tail end of another lecture from Mom and Dad.

Consequences also take the burden off the parents—kids can blame only themselves when the consequence happens. While punishment usually leads to resentment between the child and parent, consequences keep anger at bay and protect Mom and Dad from being the "bad guys."

Last but not least, consequences hold children accountable for their actions. They do so without robbing kids of dignity, in a way that's fair and effective. Trust me, your kids will suffer no ill effects of being faced with an appropriate consequence—instead they'll learn the valuable life lessons they need to know.

Consequences come in two main forms: Natural Consequences and Logical Consequences, and each is a separate tool. To meet the "fair and effective" litmus test, consequences must adhere to the 5 R's:*

---

*Adapted from Jane Nelsen, Ph.D., and H. Stephen Glenn.

- Respectful
- Related to the misbehavior, so they make sense to your child and so learning can take place without directing anger or resentment onto the parent
- Reasonable in duration based on the child's age
- Revealed in advance, so the child knows the expectation and the consequence
- Repeated to you, so you know your child is perfectly clear on the rule and the consequence

Let's dig right in so you can start putting these powerful strategies to work.

Natural Consequences

The Tool Explained

A Natural Consequence is a negative event that you allow to play out as a result of a child's repeated misbehavior. Essentially, it's what happens if you do nothing to rescue your child from his own poor choices, and it allows real life to teach your child appropriate behavior by letting him face the undesirable results of his negative actions.

For example, what if your 10-year-old constantly forgets his shin guards for soccer practice? The Natural Consequences that may play out if you don't get involved are:

- He won't be able to participate in practice.
- He'll need to face his coach with his forgetfulness.
- He'll have let his teammates down.

OUCH! As a parent, you will likely have the gut instinct to bail your son out. However, by doing so, you're robbing him of the opportunity to learn valuable life lessons like taking responsibility for his own actions, owning up to a mistake, and the importance of dependability and trust.

To be clear, we're not talking about a one-time bout of forgetfulness—anyone can make a mistake, and it's fine to help your kids when they need you. This tool is intended instead for when you notice a repeated pattern of misbehavior. Maybe your 5-year-old dawdles through dinner again and again. The Natural Consequence would be hunger an hour afterward, since you needed to clear her plate with the rest of the family's. Or your 10-year-old may consistently forget to get permission slips and other school papers signed—with Natural Consequences, he may just have to spend the duration of the cool field trip to the science museum sitting in the school library instead. In the same way, you can go ahead and let your 12-year-old wear flip-flops during a rainstorm. Her feet may get cold and wet, but that's no longer your problem.

Despite the wonderful teaching tool that Natural Consequences are, they're incredibly difficult for most parents to implement, and that's understandable. Our need to protect our kids has been developing since they were the size of a lima bean. It's instinctual, and a good thing—as long as they actually need protecting. In most of the situations we "rescue" them from, they don't. We also admittedly worry about what other adults will think. After all, the coach may know full well you live only eight minutes from the soccer field and work from home—would it really be so hard for you to deliver the shin guards? The same applies if you allow the Natural

Consequences of refusing to wear a coat play out—are you a bad parent for letting your child get cold?

Rest assured, you're doing the right thing. It's unlikely your child will go without shin guards or a coat more than once, and he'll forever have the lesson to look back on. That being said, it's often a good idea to let teachers, coaches and other activity leaders in on your plans so that they'll be able to understand, and support, your efforts.

Of course, you'll need to use common sense when considering Natural Consequences—the next tool, Logical Consequences, will help you address matters of health and safety, or times when a Natural Consequence isn't appropriate or available. For instance, you'd never let the Natural Consequences of not wearing a bike helmet or taking medication play out. You'll also want to avoid Natural Consequences if the timeline for cause and effect to play out is too long for the connection to be made, such as in the twice-a-day toothbrushing battle, and this will vary by situation and age.

Even though Natural Consequences are simple to implement, you'll need to make sure they adhere to the 5 R's so they take their course fairly and effectively:

1. *Respectful.* There's no need to humiliate or hurt your child— and if you don't deliver the Natural Consequence in a respectful, calm tone of voice, or if you allow him to face one that's above and beyond the recourse necessary, it'll feel like punishment and will be neither fair nor effective. For instance, sending your 4-year-old off to face the Natural Consequences of wearing his Superman underwear on the outside of his pants to preschool could set him up for some painful humiliation

that would take a long time to fade, and might not be the best solution for the situation. In the next tool, we'll talk about Logical Consequences you can use instead.

2. *Related.* Natural Consequences, by definition, relate to the misbehavior because they are the action's natural result. When the child refuses to eat, he's hungry later; when she wears sandals in February, she's cold; when he doesn't do his homework, he has to face the teacher and get a zero for that assignment.

3. *Reasonable.* Consider the child's age and the nature of the misbehavior when *allowing* a Natural Consequence. A consequence that is overly difficult will only induce hopelessness.

4. *Revealed in advance.* A vital part of employing Natural Consequences successfully is to make sure you inform your child that you will no longer get involved in his misbehavior, so that he's not taken by surprise (which would feel like punishment). If you've been driving shin guards to practice before now, you'll need to let your child know that the next time he forgets, it's on him. Reassure him that he's old enough to take on the responsibility of remembering his shin guards, and that you have confidence in his capabilities. All that's needed is a simple "You're mature enough to remember your shin guards for practice in the future, so I won't be reminding you or driving them to you anymore. I know you'll be able to handle this new responsibility just fine." What's more, if he does forget the shin guards and experiences the Natural Consequences, he has only himself to blame.

5. *Repeated back to you.* To be certain your child clearly understands the Natural Consequence he is facing, ask him to repeat to you the expectation and the Natural Consequences. It might

sound like "Just so we're on the same page, what are you responsible for doing, and what happens if you forget?" Now the responsibility is where it belongs—on his shoulders.

Beyond the 5 R's, you also need to remember these important ground rules:

1. *Don't rescue your child!* You need to follow through with the Natural Consequence, allowing it to play out. If you sneak your child a snack at bedtime after he's refused to eat dinner, your catering will backfire—not only will the Natural Consequence of hunger be removed, you'll instead reward the negative behavior with attention and "special service." Rest assured that after your son faces the results of his negative behavior once or twice, he won't have to deal with it again—and neither will you.

2. *Avoid piggybacking.* One of the best things about offering a Natural Consequence is that the consequence is its own lesson. There's no need for an "I told you so" of any kind, and adding insult to injury will only turn the child's anger back on you. Instead, if your child tells you, "I missed lunch today," because she forgot her lunchbox, respond with empathy: "That must have been challenging for you. How did you handle it?"

3. *Set your child up for success.* Help him find a solution to avoid the Natural Consequences in the first place, or to make sure they don't happen again. Through training or creative problem solving, you can empower your child toward better behavior in the future—possibly with a checklist of things to remember for soccer practice. And isn't that the definition of discipline?

When to Use It

- Only after employing the previous tools, to make sure your child is already feeling empowered
- When other tools to correct misbehavior either haven't worked or don't apply
- When you've found yourself consistently running to your child's rescue after he exhibits a negative behavior
- When your child is mature enough to exhibit the appropriate behavior. For instance, it may be a lot to expect a 3-year-old to remember everything she needs for preschool, so instead of allowing her to forget her lunch you could make putting it into her backpack part of her morning routine. However, an 8-year-old is more than capable.
- After you've given your child fair warning
- When the misbehavior doesn't have a health or safety risk attached to it
- For children older than 2½ (For children younger than this, use Choices or Controlling the Environment.)

Why It Works

Natural Consequences are a favorite among parents. Not only are they extremely effective when employed correctly, but they make sense to us and to our kids.

With Natural Consequences, life becomes the teacher. Unlike a contrived and ineffective discipline tool such as a time-out, they teach real lessons, so that when a child is deciding how to behave in the future, he'll have a true experience of his own to look back on. This is empowering to the child—even though he learned a tough lesson, it was on his own terms.

Natural Consequences also make the child responsible for herself. Let's face it—while our kids might outwardly appreciate being rescued by their parents, it comes with a sense of embarrassment and disappointment. Even though being held accountable is never pleasant, the child will soon feel a sense of accomplishment for her better behavior in the future. And having been exposed to life's realities in a safe environment during childhood, she'll be better prepared for the consequences she'll encounter as an independent adult—such as the fact that neglecting to pay your phone bill renders that fancy new cell phone useless.

By removing ourselves from the situation, we as parents not only feel a burden lifted (do any of us actually enjoy driving shin guards to practice, or nagging our children so that they'll remember?), but we can help our kids learn from their mistakes without being the focus of their anger. Even if they're upset, they know they have no one to blame but themselves. And that's a very freeing thought for a parent.

Tips for Success
- Use your Calm Voice and the Parent Ego State as you communicate with your child. A Natural Consequence shouldn't be delivered in anger or in the heat of the moment. It should never be "Put on your coat, for heaven's sake, or you'll freeze to death!" as they run out the door.
- Adopt an attitude of indifference about your child's choice in the consequence. Remember that it's a win-win situation—either your child will make the right choice, or learn from the wrong one.
- Once you've told your child that he'll be responsible for his own actions in this particular situation, don't mention it again. Part

of learning appropriate behavior includes not needing to be reminded or told what to do.

- Once you've revealed the consequence in advance, help set your child up for success. If it's a matter of remembering homework or gym clothes for school, for instance, you can prompt him with "What can you use to help you remember these, since I won't be reminding you?" The solution might be a list posted by the door, or a laminated card in the soccer bag listing the items needed for practice. The goal is for your child to be successful, but you can help with training and controlling the environment.

- Follow through! Otherwise, not only will your child learn nothing from her mistakes, but she'll see that you don't mean what you say.

- Partner with other people who may become involved, such as the librarian at your child's elementary school or a youth group leader, so that they know what's going on and can support your efforts. Shoot them a quick e-mail that says something like "Carston is working on remembering his library books by himself, without reminders from his parents. If he forgets to return them on time, he's prepared to handle the consequences you have in place." This will help ensure that 7-year-old Carston will face the appropriate Natural Consequences set up by his library—and not be let off the hook for his sweet dimpled smile.

Logical Consequences

The Tool Explained

Logical Consequences are used when Natural Consequences aren't available or practical, such as in matters of health and safety (wearing a bike helmet or taking medication), or if a Natural Consequence would take so long to play out that the lesson would be lost (not brushing teeth). A Logical Consequence is engineered by the parent, but it should still relate directly to the misbehavior so that your child can easily make a cause-and-effect connection.

You can develop a Logical Consequence by denying or delaying a privilege, or by requiring your child to make amends, such as cleaning up the mashed potatoes she threw at dinner, or drawing a picture for the child she hurt while roughhousing at a playdate. As with Natural Consequences, you'll need to establish the Logical Consequence in advance, and it's essential you follow the 5 R's to make sure your Logical Consequence is both fair and effective:

1. *Respectful.* If your Logical Consequence isn't respectful, it'll feel like punishment and will be neither fair nor effective. In the case of your 4-year-old who wants to wear his Superman underwear on the outside of his pants (just like Superman!), it might be a better strategy to let him change in the parking lot before going into preschool once the novelty wears off and he realizes that unless you can fly, you get made fun of for such things.

2. *Related.* Denying your child dessert certainly isn't going to teach your child not to jump on the living room couch—but having

to vacuum the cushions since he messed them up with his horse-play probably would. And it makes much more logical sense to deny your child the privilege of riding her bike if she won't wear a helmet than to make her miss the sleepover that night. Keep the consequence related to the misdeed, or you'll confuse your child and muddle the lesson he needs to learn. The more closely you can relate the two, the more effective the lesson will be.

3. *Reasonable.* Adjust your expectations and the consequence according to your child's maturity level, to make sure the correct behavior is achievable and the Logical Consequence isn't overly harsh (or lenient). If your 10-year-old refuses to complete her family contribution of folding the towels when they come out of the dryer, for example, it'd be too much to expect her to be responsible for the entire family's laundry for a week as a consequence—but it'd be too little to let her get away with simply hauling the basket upstairs so you can do it. Because she created an inconvenience for you, it would be a reasonable consequence to add one of your normal tasks to her contribution list, such as folding the white clothes and distributing them to each person's room.

4. *Revealed in advance.* Inform your child of the Logical Consequences you've put in place, including what your expectation or rule is, and the consequence for not following the rule. If she chooses to endure the Logical Consequence instead of behaving appropriately, she has only herself to blame.

5. *Repeated to you.* To be certain your child clearly understands the Logical Consequence you're giving him, he should repeat the expectation or rule and the consequence to you after you've communicated them to him in advance.

Logical Consequences can be tricky to develop at first, so here are a few examples.

For a 5-year-old who won't brush her teeth, the Natural Consequence of enduring the dentist's drill isn't practical. Cavities wouldn't likely appear until much later—not to mention the fact that they can mean bad news for a child's overall health and your family's budget. Instead, you could employ a Logical Consequence to restrict your child from eating any type of sugar—whether candy bars, fruit or Goldfish crackers—as the alternative way to avoid dental problems. A steady diet of only protein and vegetables will soon solve the problem, if the Logical Consequence even gets that far. In a calm moment, say, "I understand you don't want to brush your teeth and I can't force you to brush them. However, we'll have to adjust your diet to prevent cavities. You can have food from the vegetable group, the dairy group and the protein group on the food pyramid, but you'll need to stay away from sugar, fruits and the breads and grains group unless you brush your teeth twice a day."

A kindergartener who throws puzzle pieces might lose the privilege of playing with the puzzle for the rest of the day as a Logical Consequence: "Our rule is that the puzzle pieces have to stay on the table. If you choose to throw the puzzle pieces or not treat them gently, they will be put away for the rest of the day." In the same way, a 13-year-old who is texting before homework is finished would lose his phone privileges for the week. You'd simply say, "Our rule is that homework must be completed before using your phone each day. If you aren't able to follow that rule, you're telling us you're not mature enough to handle the responsibilities of having a cell phone and you'll lose your phone and texting privileges for one week."

When to Use It

- Only after empowering your children by using the tools in the previous chapters
- Only when Natural Consequences don't apply and the previous tools can't or don't address the issue
- When dealing with a repeated misbehavior
- When you are able to develop an effective Logical Consequence, using the 5 R's, that makes sense (If you can't think of one, this might not be the right tool.)
- When your child is mature enough to exhibit the appropriate behavior
- After you've given your child fair warning
- For children older than 2½ (For children younger than this, use Choices and Controlling the Environment.)

Why It Works

Logical Consequences work effectively for many of the same reasons Natural Consequences do: They make your kids responsible for their actions, they show kids a direct result of misbehavior and they let children maintain a sense of dignity as they learn real-life lessons.

And even though parents have to involve themselves a bit more with Logical Consequences than with Natural ones, the parent is still removed from the situation to a certain extent, allowing the child to choose for himself whether he wants to continue the misbehavior or endure the consequence. However, because the parent has to create the Logical Consequence and also enforce it, this tool isn't quite as powerful as the Natural Consequences tool, so it should be used only when Natural Consequences aren't possible.

Tips for Success

- Your Logical Consequence must include the 5 R's or it will feel like punishment, turning the child's anger on you. Consequences aren't about making the child suffer, they're about helping the child learn to make a better choice in the future.

- Always communicate with a Calm Voice and from a Parent Ego State and adopt an attitude of indifference. Be unconcerned with which choice your child makes and let your child make the decision for herself.

- Say the consequence one time—no repeating or reminding. If you continue to remind your child, there's no need for your child to remember on his own.

- If your child makes a poor choice, follow through with dignity and respect, and calmly implement the consequence. Again, there's no need for a lecture or an "I told you so." As long as you used the 5 R's, the consequence will teach the lesson without you being the bad guy.

- It may aid your efforts to partner with your child's caregiver, instructor or anyone else who may become involved in the Logical Consequence. They can help make sure the appropriate consequence is carried out, and they're usually more than happy to help.

Which to Choose?

One of the most common questions I get from parents about consequences is how to know which one to choose. Here are my guidelines:

In matters of health and safety, you'll almost always need to choose a Logical Consequence. Beyond that, you'll need to decide based on who is most affected (or inconvenienced, or bothered) by the problem if it's allowed to play out. If the child will be most affected, use a Natural Consequence. In Bella's case from the example in the beginning of the chapter, although she's passing the problem off to her mother, she's actually the one naturally affected by her forgetfulness. Without her mom coming to her rescue, Bella is the one who will have to face the librarian with overdue books, or borrow money to buy lunch. Bella's mom would be wise to reveal the Natural Consequences in advance and then sit back and do nothing the next time Bella forgets something—once the Natural Consequences play out, Bella's forgetfulness will likely disappear as if by magic.

On the other hand, a child who acts up in a restaurant isn't usually affected by his misbehavior, but his parents certainly are. Instead of enjoying their meal, they're wrangling a child who's throwing food or running in circles, and all the while enduring the annoyed glances of fellow diners. Since there's no Natural Consequence that fits in this situation (the child is probably having a good time misbehaving and isn't likely to face a negative result), the parents will need to use a Logical Consequence that they've developed. The Logical Consequence could be to leave the restaurant, or sit in the car (with a parent) until everyone else is done eating. No, this won't be convenient for you in either case—but it's important that you're willing to sacrifice short-term enjoyment (like finishing your grilled salmon)—for the long-term benefits of teaching a valuable lesson. Remember, you set up the Logical Consequence for a reason, so you need to be committed to following through. You'll enjoy your salmon that much more the next time.

If you can't think of a Natural or Logical Consequence that

makes sense and that meets the 5 R's of fair and effective consequences, you need to let it go and try something else entirely. For instance, a parent once asked me what to do with a young child who continually ran away from her in stores, airports and other public places. She couldn't think of any kind of consequence to use. As it turned out, the child simply needed more training in proper behavior while shopping. They created a "stop in your tracks" maneuver for when the boy saw something so exciting he "had" to see it, and they role-played a variety of situations. Soon the child knew exactly what was expected of him—and the misbehavior disappeared. In this case, the most effective tool to solve the problem was Take Time for Training, and consequences were unnecessary.

As you begin to use consequences, continue to employ the other tools you've learned as well. By laying the proper groundwork with strategies like Make When-Then Routines the Boss, or Control the Environment, you shouldn't have to resort to consequences too often. If you find yourself turning to consequences fairly often, you may need to reevaluate your tactics to make sure you're providing your kids with enough positive attention throughout the day, sufficient opportunities to exercise positive power, and the training they need to act correctly. The final tool in this chapter is a type of consequence that comes into play when a misbehavior requires your immediate attention and a When-Then or Choice isn't available. It's called an Either-Or, and it's for those times when you need to quickly put an end to a negative action without turning it into a power struggle.

Consequences and Family Contributions

· ·

Having trouble getting your kids to complete their family contributions? If a When-Then or a When-Then Routine hasn't worked or doesn't apply in your situation, you may need to implement consequences. For instance, if a child's contribution is to pick up her room by five every afternoon, an appropriate consequence could be to move anything left lying around at that time to a box in the garage for two days. Or for a child who refuses to empty the dishwasher, his consequence would add an additional contribution: dealing with all of the dishes that have piled up in the sink as a result of his negligence. As with any consequence, make sure you reveal it in advance.

TOOLBOX SOLUTION #12

Either-Or Consequences

The Tool Explained

Either-Or Consequences are a type of Logical Consequence designed to give a quick and simple consequence-based choice to kids that will put an end to a misbehavior without inviting a power struggle. You can use these consequences as a misbehavior is happening, in the heat of the moment.

An Either-Or Consequence might be used, for instance, if your 9-year-old won't relinquish the computer when her Internet time is up for the day. An appropriate Either-Or Consequence might sound like this: "*Either* you sign off the computer now, *or* you'll lose Internet privileges for three days—no IM'ing, games, e-mail or anything else." For younger kids who are fighting over a toy, you could say: "*Either* you two need to figure out how to share the toy, *or* the toy will go in a box in the closet and no one will be allowed to play with it for a week." Most of the time your children will comply, but if they don't, follow through with the consequence.

As you construct and communicate an Either-Or Consequence, make sure it follows the 5 R's: it needs to be respectful, related to the misbehavior, reasonable, revealed in advance (as the negative behavior is occurring, but before you would follow through on it) and repeated back to you. Just as when using When-Then, emphasize the words *either* and *or* as you say them so that your kids can begin to predict what's coming—they should soon learn that when you phrase a sentence this way, they need to take notice.

When to Use It

- As a negative behavior is happening, for which you have not already set up a Natural or Logical Consequence
- Only when none of the previous tools apply
- For children over age 2½

Why It Works

An Either-Or Consequence is like a mini-consequence. It addresses a misbehavior through cause and effect; however, it's not thought out in advance like a Natural or Logical Consequence would be. It also resembles a When-Then or Choices in its ability to stop a power struggle in its tracks by giving kids the control they're seeking, on your terms. With an Either-Or Consequence, that means allowing kids the power to choose to experience the direct result of their negative actions, which you've revealed in advance.

Since it takes on characteristics of all these tools, an Either-Or Consequence works for the same reasons. It gives responsibility and power to your children, helping them learn from their behavior and removing you from the situation so that there's no way to argue or negotiate.

Tips for Success

- Not sure if you should use a When-Then or an Either-Or? As a rule of thumb, a When-Then should be used when you want your child *to do* something: "*When* you finish folding your laundry, *then* we can leave for the park." An Either-Or can be used when you want your child to *stop* doing something: "*Either* you can stop roughhousing in the house, *or* you can go outside and play."
- State the Either-Or clearly, and only once. Your child should then have all the information he needs to make the right decision.
- Do not respond with an Either-Or out of anger, or it will feel like a punishment. Use your Calm Voice and the Adult Ego State, and act indifferent about the outcome.
- Follow through with the *or* part of your consequence if your child makes the inappropriate choice.

Consequences of all types are powerful and will get results. They're a positive way to approach challenging misbehaviors with your child. However, it's important not to overuse them. Our goal is to empower our kids to make the right choices and learn the appropriate behavior—and the best way to do this is to set our kids on the right path using the positive tools in previous chapters. Tools #1 through #9 should correct about eighty-five percent of the misbehavior under your roof. For the remaining misbehaviors, favor Natural Consequences ahead of Logical Consequences, as your kids will learn the lesson more successfully if the results of their negative actions can play out through real life, with minimal interference on your part.

Mini-Tool: Stop Talking and Take Action

Think about this: If kids learned from our words, they'd always mind their manners, never jump on the couch and remember their lunchboxes every single day. But that doesn't exactly describe any child I know! In fact, kids learn from our actions—and that's why we need to focus on taking consistent action whenever a misbehavior strikes, without speaking at all. Here's how:

First, train your child in the expected behavior, and reveal the consequence for not following the rule. After that, there's no need to say another word.

If the misbehavior happens, calmly implement the action you revealed in advance. If your child has a meltdown, ignore it and walk away (as long as your child is in a safe place). Handling a meltdown can be particularly tricky in public, whether you're slogging through the grocery store or dining in a crowded restaurant. In these instances, calmly pick up your child or lead her by the hand to retreat outside, or to your car, until she can quiet down.

The Stop Talking and Take Action mini-tool relies on your silence to make it effective. Reminding your child over and over what kind of behavior is expected will only make her parent-deaf, which happens when kids learn to tune out your words because there's no real reason to listen. For instance, a toddler in a sandbox doesn't need forty-two reminders not to throw sand. Once you've revealed the consequence in advance, simply remove the child from the sandbox each and every time he tosses a handful, calmly and without saying a word. Or, if your kids are acting up at the dinner table, just take away their plates and let them know they're excused—no reminders necessary once you've let them know you won't put up with dinner disruptions.

Stop Talking and Take Action works because it lets kids know that we're serious. We don't act in anger, but we do take action. Remember to remain calm as you act, as getting upset will only invite a power struggle.

With less talking and more action, your kids will soon learn that you mean business—and take you at your *first* word.

Revisiting Bella

Revisiting Bella's forgetfulness at the beginning of the chapter, here's how the story could've played out if Bella's parents had used some positive strategies, including Natural Consequences, to train her to be more mindful of what she needs for school.

IT WOULD seem that Bella is just about the most forgetful girl in her third-grade class. She's kind to her peers, she pays attention and her work is above average, and yet several times a week Bella's mom pops her head into the classroom with a forgotten lunch, rain boots, library books, a permission slip, an interesting seashell for show-and-tell, mittens—even Bella's shoes one time when she accidentally made it all the way to school without changing out of her pink bunny slippers.

Bella's parents decide it's time to train her to remember her own belongings—without constant reminders. They sit down with Bella and outline a plan.

"What would help you remember everything you need for school?" asks Bella's dad.

"Um . . . I don't know," replies Bella.

"Well, how about you make a list of the things you need to take every day and put it somewhere that you could see it often?"

"Yeah, I think that would help a lot!" Bella replies.

"We could put it in the kitchen so you can check it after dinner and before breakfast," her mom offers.

"And how about a special cubby to put all your school things in, so they're not just sitting by the door?" suggests Bella's dad.

"Cool! We use those at school!" Bella agrees.

"And I think it would help the whole family if we set up a routine for school mornings. Then we can all take the time to make sure we each have everything we need."

"Okay," says Bella.

Bella and her parents get started. They write a list of things Bella needs for each day of the week, depending on what she may have going on at or after school (gym class, field trip, a violin lesson). Together, they develop two simple routines—one for nighttime and one for morning—that include time for Bella to review her list and gather her things for school. Finally, they find a cubby for Bella's school things that she decorates with stickers.

They also make sure to reveal natural consequences: "Remember," Bella's mom tells her, "this means I won't be reminding you about bringing your things to school, and I won't be driving them to you. Our plan should help you get everything you need, but if you forget, you'll need to figure it out on your own. Just to make sure you understand, can you repeat back what I just said?"

Bella repeats back, "You won't be reminding me to pack my things for school, and you won't drive them to me if I forget, so I need to remember by myself. And if I forget, I have to figure out what to do. But what if I get in trouble with my teacher?!"

"Well, that could happen, but you'll need to face that possibility," says Bella's mom. "And I have full confidence that you can remember on your own!"

With the plan in place, Bella remembers everything she needs for school the next couple of days—and feels great about herself. On Friday, however, she forgets to bring her gym shoes. She glumly tells her mom about it when she gets home.

"That's too bad, sweetie! What did you do during gym class?"

"Elizabeth let me borrow hers, but they pinched so I couldn't run very fast. I was the first one caught in Capture the Flag."

"Do you think you'll remember next time, or do we need to adjust the plan," asks Bella's mom.

"Oh, I think I'll remember! But I'm going to go put them in my cubby right now, just in case!"

———————

WITH the training tools you have now, you're well on your way to raising kids that are empowered through strong senses of belonging and significance toward positive actions. The next few chapters will address some more targeted—and very relevant—concerns, beginning with a look at some of the misguided goals your child may be pursuing when she misbehaves.

FAQs

What should I do when a misbehavior happens that I didn't anticipate, so I didn't reveal a consequence in advance?

You shouldn't use consequences if you haven't revealed them in advance. Instead, use the misbehavior as a teaching moment and take the opportunity to train your child in the right behavior for the situation. If it seems that the misbehavior will become a repeated one, you can go ahead and set up consequences after the first incident so that next time you can implement them. You can also use Either-Or Consequences, if the situation calls for it.

My child misbehaved at school and she's already faced a consequence. Do I need to also give her a consequence when she gets home?

That's not necessary—she's already faced her consequence and doesn't need another one. It'll be much more helpful to your child (and her teacher) for you to talk with her about the misbehavior, and ask what she'd do differently next time. You can even role-play the situation until your child feels comfortable with the appropriate behavior. This is a much more effective way to change negative behavior long term than simply to issue another consequence.

What happens if I can't think of a consequence for a misbehavior?
If you can't think of a consequence that meets the 5 R's—respectful, related to the misbehavior, reasonable, revealed in advance and re-peated back—let it go. It probably means that a consequence is not called for. Instead, go back to the Toolbox and use another tool such as Mind, Body & Soul Time, Take Time for Training, Choices, When-Then Routines and the like. Remember, consequ-ences should be used only about fifteen percent of the time.

What's an appropriate consequence for harming another person?
Whether your child hurts someone physically or emotionally, on purpose or by accident, an excellent Logical Consequence is to ask him what he needs to do to *make it right* with the other person, beyond the obligatory "I'm sorry." A hug, a note or another act of kindness is certainly in order—and chances are it will make both parties feel better. Your child will also develop a stronger sense of empathy and personal responsibility in the long run.

EXAMPLES OF MISBEHAVIORS AND CONSEQUENCES

Misbehavior	Natural or Logical?	Consequence Example
Refusing to do homework/ denying there's any homework to do	Natural	Child has to face the teacher the next day and potentially lose credit for the assignment.
Refusing to pick up toys	Logical	Toys that are not picked up before bedtime will be put in a box at the back of the basement and will be unavailable for two days.
Wanting to put too much stuff in backpack	Natural	Backpack is heavy.
Bossing friends around, or cheating when playing games/sports with them	Natural	Friends will not want to play with him.
Refusing to change out of good clothes	Logical	Child will have to stay in the house and find a quiet, nonmessy activity until he changes his clothes.
Leaving toys out in the yard	Logical	Child loses the privilege of playing with those toys for a certain period of time.
Spending allowance foolishly	Natural	Child will have no money when he wants to buy something important and will have to wait until he has enough money saved.
Staying up too late and running late for school	Natural	Child is tired the next day, and has to face teacher and accept school-imposed consequences for tardiness.

THE FOUR MISTAKEN
GOALS OF MISBEHAVIOR

Owen's dad, Paul, works from home part-time. It's an arrange-ment that's allowed him to spend most of his days in close proximity to Owen since the boy was born four years ago, and yet still have a work life—when Owen lets him, anyway.

Today, Owen is headed off to preschool—a biweekly occur-rence ever since the September when Owen was three years old. And yet, it's always a struggle.

"Put on your shoes, grab your bag and let's hop in the car—I'll race you!" Paul says brightly, hoping Owen will adopt his enthusi-asm and accept the challenge. He works on gathering up a few papers he needs to drop off at the office after Owen's at school, and puts a lid on his coffee mug.

Meanwhile, Owen fiddles listlessly with his shoelaces.

"Are you coming, son? I've just about got my shoes on!"

"Put mine on, Daddy. I can't do it," pleads Owen, who has recently learned with great success to tie his own shoes.

Paul checks his watch. It's getting late, and he really needs to have the papers dropped off shortly after nine. He decides he can put Owen's shoes on just this once, and stoops to help his son.

"All right, let's go!" he says.

"Wait—I forgot Dino!" Owen panics.

Paul checks his son's backpack, and sure enough, there's no orange dinosaur in sight.

"Hold on, I'll get him," says Paul as he rushes up the stairs to Owen's room. The dinosaur is feasting on space aliens in the corner, right where Owen left him last night.

"Okay, into the car, we're late!" says Paul.

"Can I wear my baseball cap?" asks Owen.

"Fine. Here you go." Paul grabs the cap from its hook and shoves it on Owen's head.

The phone rings. It's Paul's boss, and he has to take the call. Fortunately, he has a mute button, and his boss is the one who usually does all the talking.

Owen catches his dad's eye, silently pointing to the fridge and whispering, "Apple?"

Paul opens the fridge and gets the apple, and then points to the car. Owen finally edges out the door, and Paul is soon able to answer his boss's quick question and hang up the phone.

Paul locks up, pulls the garbage can and recycle bin to the curb and heads for the car. Owen is now back at the door, ringing the doorbell over and over again.

"Daddy, help me open the door!"

"What do you need *now*?" asks Paul, exasperated.

"Um, I think Baxter wants to come, too. Can we bring him?" Owen begs. Baxter is the family poodle, and Paul is confident that he'd much rather nap on the screened porch than go for a ride all over town.

"No." Paul lays down the law. "Into the car." He opens Owen's car door.

"But he's lonely! Let's play with him, just for one minute."

"We're already late!" Paul says.

Owen reluctantly settles into his booster seat while Paul starts the engine.

"Are you buckled?" Paul leans back to double-check. Owen hasn't even begun.

"The straps are twisted," Owen comments. "Can you do it?"

Paul quickly buckles Owen into his seat (the straps are only very mildly twisted) and gets ready to pull out of the driveway. Then, "Uh-oh," he hears from the backseat, much to his dismay.

"What?" he asks.

"I dropped Dino!"

And so it continues. Paul manages to convince Owen that he doesn't actually have to go potty, and that he'll have a snack at preschool, and that there are no monsters in the car's trunk, but the duo is still already fifteen minutes behind schedule for the day.

Getting out the door is just the beginning. All day, every day, Owen's constant badgering renders Paul almost helpless to finish a conversation, cook dinner or sit down and check his e-mail. Whether it's "Play with me!" or "Did you know that butterflies come from caterpillars?" or "My toy needs batteries," Owen sometimes seems more high-maintenance now than when he was a newborn. Paul has always kept hoping this is something Owen will eventually grow out of. And he's been expecting that to happen for the past four years.

The Root of the Problem

Sometimes, our kids' misbehaviors appear as a tiny blip in their lives. One week Gracie is hiding cheese cubes in houseplants (for the ladybugs to eat), and by the next week, she's lost interest. Roberto turns his music up much too loud—but only once, having stopped the first time you used an Either-Or. Maybe you've been running errands all day with 2½-year-old Makayla, she's missed her nap and has finished all her snacks, and now she's having the king of all tantrums on the floor of your favorite department store, but can you blame her?

Other times, the patterns continue for weeks, months or, if left unchecked, years. Maybe your needy newborn turns into a clingy toddler and a badgering, interrupting child, like Owen. Or maybe lately it's seemed that the 8-year-old in the family provokes you to your limit, on purpose. It could be that you're facing misbehaviors even more extreme, possibly in the form of a destructive preteen who seems to be out to get you, or a child who seems to have given up on herself.

It's these behaviors that should compel us to reflect on a greater, underlying issue. We know we have a problem—but where's its root? Only when we uncover the motives for the repeated negative behavior can we address our children's deepest needs and solve a host of misbehaviors at the same time.

We've clearly established that our kids' misbehavior is always related to their inherent requirements for a sense of belonging and a sense of significance. Everything comes back to these primary emotional goals, and you've probably begun to see just how important they are as you implement the tools we've covered.

Now it's time to go one step further, and explore the four ways in which your kids mistakenly believe they can achieve positive attention and positive power—or other more desperate goals— through their misbehavior.

With each mistaken goal, you have a child who is trying to find what they're seeking in the wrong way, because of an errant belief. For instance, a child may think she can find the sense of power she's looking for by drawing her dad into a power struggle every time he asks for her help around the house. She wants to assert herself and win the battle, believing she can build her sense of significance this way. Of course, she can't articulate her feelings, but by evaluating her behavior we can determine what she's trying to do.

Children with mistaken goals will end up receiving negative attention or power instead of positive, but will settle for it because they've developed tried-and-true strategies for receiving it. They've found something that works, and negative is better than nothing.

THERE ARE four mistaken goals of misbehavior, and they're progressive—the first leads to the next, and so on. Here's each one in a nutshell:

1. *Undue Attention.* A child whines, badgers, interrupts, clings, demands special service or acts helpless simply to get his

parents' attention in a misapplied attempt to gain a sense of belonging.

2. *Power.* A child challenges or provokes a parent, with the goal of initiating a power struggle that she can "win," and in so doing, gain a sense of significance.

3. *Revenge.* A child has found he can't achieve a sense of belonging or significance, and instead just tries to get even with his parents by inflicting physical or emotional harm.

4. *Assumed Inadequacy.* Having failed in all previous goals, the child now gives up, detaches and wants to be left alone.*

We'll cover each of these in more detail, and introduce some tools and strategies for handling them. But first, let's get to the bottom of how the mistaken goals develop. We'll have to dig up a little dirt in the process.

The Dirt Surrounding the Root of the Problem

The patterns of misbehavior you see with mistaken goals don't simply appear—they're created over time. For instance, Owen wasn't born a clingy preschooler, but through trial and error he learned that the more he badgered his busy dad, the more time his dad gave him, even if just in fifteen-second "fixes" between calls and e-mails.

Owen's mistaken goal is clearly Undue Attention. Despite the fact that his dad is around and relatively available almost all day long, Owen constantly demands more of Paul's mindshare.

---

*Adapted from Rudolf Dreikurs, M.D., *Children: The Challenge* (Plume/Penguin, 1990).

But why? Paul asks himself this question all the time: "I'm with Owen *all day, every day!* How can he possibly still need more of my attention?" This mistaken goal could stem from a lot of things: It probably has something to do with the way Owen is wired, and something to do with the habits he's grown accustomed to, and a lot to do with how Paul responds to Owen's appeals for attention.

The important thing is to understand how mistaken goals take shape. Once we know the root cause, we can begin to correct the misbehavior.

Looking back again at Adlerian psychology, we'll remember that all behavior is goal-oriented. Kids are motivated to act a certain way because they have learned through trial and error that their actions will achieve a certain result. So, to decode behavior like Owen's, we simply need to look at our response immediately following the negative behavior to determine what Owen's goal is. As we've seen, Paul's reaction is to almost always acknowledge Owen's request, and often to grant it—and in the meantime, focus on Owen exclusively. Looks like Owen's accomplishing his goal of getting Paul's attention almost flawlessly! The same goes for the other mistaken goals: Our kids have figured out how to get the response from us that they want—even if it's negative—which turns a quest for more attention, power or revenge, or just a desire to be left alone, into a repeated action.

Owen's mistaken belief is that he'll receive the positive attention he needs by badgering his dad. He doesn't have the mental capacity to realize that what he really wants is quality time (as opposed to a few seconds of negative attention), let alone the emotional maturity to say, "Daddy, I know you're at home all day long, but you're always busy doing something else! I want us to spend some time together when you don't have your phone out or your computer in front of you!" Instead, what passes through Owen's mind is something like "If I ask Daddy to button my shirt for me, he'll pay attention to me!" Which, when verbalized, comes out as "Daddy, I can't do the buttons!" An annoyed Paul fastens Owen's buttons and then turns away, but Owen has accomplished what he wanted—and he's had his tactic reinforced so he'll be even more likely to present a similar request in the future.

Mistaken goals of misbehavior are progressive, so that if parents leave them unaddressed or continually respond negatively—such as with punishment—each will lead to the next. So, if Owen's demands for attention are not met in positive ways, he is likely to resort to the next mistaken goal, Power. If Owen's new assortment of Power-seeking behaviors are consistently met with punishment, he will likely begin to want Revenge, with a newfound determination to get even. And if Paul still continues to administer punishment, Owen may eventually decide it's no use to even try to achieve a positive sense of belonging and significance, and give up entirely, just as in the mistaken goal of Assumed Inadequacy.

Diagnosing a Mistaken Goal

To determine *which* mistaken goal you're dealing with requires a little detective work. First, take a look at your reaction. How do you feel when the misbehavior happens? What do you naturally do as a result of the misbehavior? Then, evaluate your child's response *after* you've responded. Essentially, what's her reaction to your re-action, once the misbehavior takes place? Once you've evaluated these things, the chart below will then help you decode your child's mistaken goal.*

Mistaken Goal	Typical Signs or Misbehaviors	Parent's Reaction	Child's Response
Undue Attention	Interrupting, clinging, whining, acting helpless	Feels irritated and annoyed. Likely to reprimand or cave in.	Feels satisfied in the short term, but usually engages in a similar misbehavior (seeking attention) in the very near future
Power	Refusing to cooperate, back-talking, tantrums, badgering, negotiating	Feels angry, challenged or provoked. Likely to engage in a power struggle, reprimand, raise voice or punish.	Raises voice and escalates the situation when parent reprimands. Doesn't give in.
Revenge	Physical damage, emotional hurt	Feels hurt or in disbelief. May feel compelled to respond with punishment.	Retaliates with worse behavior next time. Ups his response each episode.
Assumed Inadequacy	Giving up, becoming withdrawn.	Feels desperate, extremely discouraged, at a loss. May give up on the child, or continue to punish.	Gives up, pretends not to care or acts helpless. Withdraws from parental contact.

And of course you'd be remiss not to scope out the situation as a whole. If you're pouring a glass of milk for yourself and your daughter asks if you can pour one for her, too, she's probably not seeking Undue Attention—she likely just wants a glass of milk and is asking something perfectly reasonable since you have the milk

---

*The chart is adapted from Jane Nelsen, *Positive Discipline* (New York: Ballantine Books, 2006), p. 71.

in your hand. However, if you're on the phone and the milk is in the fridge, her request for you to pour her a glass of milk is likely Undue Attention. You can determine it as such because you're feeling irritated or annoyed: "Can't she see I'm on the phone?" If your son is extra clingy because he's sick, that's also not Undue Attention. However, if he's perfectly healthy but wants to be picked up all the time or demands your constant attention to the point of irritation and annoyance, it's likely Undue Attention, and you'll know because of how you feel. Undue Attention always falls outside the bounds of what is reasonable in a particular situation.

A 7-year-old who refuses to eat peas because they make her gag is not doing so because she's seeking power. However, if you have to coax and nag her to eat every night—no matter what you're serving—she may be on a power-seeking mission. And a 3-year-old who's having a meltdown tantrum at the eighth store you've visited that day is not engaged in a power struggle. But if he consistently throws a fit when he doesn't get his way, that could signify a power problem.

Likewise, if your 3-year-old is suddenly hitting kids at playgroup or throwing blocks, he's probably not on a rampage to get revenge. He's probably just a 3-year-old undergoing a typical, albeit difficult, phase. If your 11-year-old, though, throws your cell phone into the sink with the dishes you're washing, it's likely she's acting out of revenge.

And the sixth-grader who suddenly needs his own space might not be withdrawing for any reason other than that he's no longer your little boy. On the other hand, an 8-year-old who won't open up about anything and just wants to be left alone for days or weeks on end could be experiencing Assumed Inadequacy.

Once you diagnose a mistaken goal, you'll need to address it as soon as possible. Your child is on a mission, and her behavior isn't random—there's a real underlying issue, with a real goal. If you don't determine what the issue is and begin implementing a solution, the misbehavior will only escalate and progress. It's your job to make sure your child receives the positive sense of belonging and significance he needs, and also to put an end to the misbehavior.

With each mistaken goal, there are strategies to use in the moment, and long-term strategies as well, to solve the underlying problem and prevent future outbreaks. The key thing to remember is that because the misbehavior is continuing, you're contributing to it in some way. Therefore, to solve the misbehavior, in most cases you'll need to react contrary to your gut instinct, and often in the *opposite* way you normally would. Remember, your child is receiving the payoff she's aiming for through your current response, so only by trying something completely different will you get the results you're looking for.

Careful analysis will help you apply the tools you've learned, and the five additional ones we'll cover in this chapter, to help your child learn that she *can* receive the positive attention and power she's aiming for, but without the misbehavior.

We'll cover each mistaken goal on its own in the upcoming sections, beginning with the first: Undue Attention.

Mistaken Goal #1: Undue Attention

As the first mistaken goal—and the one that most often jump-starts the progression of misbehavior—Undue Attention plagues a lot of families. Even if we feel like we're already giving our kids a lot of attention, they may still want more. And for those of us who have been a little too busy to spend consistent one-on-one time with our children, we may feel guilty—but there's still misbehavior to correct as we mend our own ways.

Owen's story is obviously one of Undue Attention. The signature misbehaviors include interrupting, whining, clinging, acting helpless and demanding endless acts of service ("Mommy, my cup fell, can you pick it up?"). While a 2-year-old may constantly beg to be played with, picked up or unnecessarily helped using a spoon, a 12-year-old might interrupt all of your conversations, enlist your aid with math problems you know she can handle or complain about anything and everything.

Of course, many kids exhibit these behaviors from time to time—are they all pursuing the mistaken goal of Undue Attention? The request for attention is undue if it happens repeatedly, and there's a pattern of similar misbehaviors. Also, it's undue if:

1. You feel irritated or annoyed.
2. Your child is satisfied for a short time, but soon tries to get your attention again.

Take Owen, for instance. He made Paul jump through every hoop in the book to complete the simple task of heading out the door to preschool. Not only did leaving the house take twice as long as it should have, but Owen managed to secure Paul's attention for almost the entire time. And Paul played into it—he would do anything if it'd bring him one step closer to being on the road. Accordingly, this happens every preschool morning, and throughout the day. Why? Because it works!

To address Undue Attention, you'll need some strategies to use as the misbehavior is happening, and some that will correct and prevent the misbehavior long term. The only way to put an end to Undue Attention misbehaviors in the moment is to quit providing a payoff—which means to ignore every undue request. This technique is covered in greater detail in the next Toolbox Solution.

The most important tool for clearing up the misbehaviors long term is, of course, Mind, Body & Soul Time. Make sure you give your child positive attention throughout the day, so she won't feel the need to seek it—mistakenly—on her own. Regular use of Encouragement will also help, as well as a technique I call Attention Overload, which is Toolbox Solution #14.

It's vital that you address both the short-term misbehaviors and the long-term underlying problem. If you try simply for a "quick fix" as the misbehaviors are happening, and neglect to offer your child plenty of positive attention to replace the negative attention she's been receiving, the situation will only escalate, and your child will likely begin Power-seeking behaviors as well—the second mistaken goal of misbehavior. Remember that every child, no matter her age or disposition, needs to feel a sense of belonging and significance. When you help her gain these, many misbehaviors—not just those attributed to mistaken goals—will simply disappear.

Ignore Undue-Attention Requests

The Tool Explained

Addressing misbehaviors associated with the mistaken goal of Undue Attention is done simply by ignoring the misbehavior, whether it's a demand for help with something the child can do himself, or constant clinginess every time you need to concentrate on a task at hand. But to completely ignore your child's best attempts to garner your attention can be easier said than done. This tool will provide the method and some helpful tips.

Here's what to do:

1. Reveal in advance what you're going to do, keeping in mind your child's age and maturity. You can use the Decide What *You* Will Do tool to control your response to your child. Inform him: "Whining hurts my ears. I will no longer pay any attention to you when you use your whiny voice. When you talk to me in your normal voice, I'll be happy to talk to you." Or, "When I'm cooking dinner, I'm not available to play with you. When you beg me to play with you while I'm making dinner, I'm going to ignore the request."

2. Train your child in the appropriate behavior. Help your child learn what constitutes acceptable behavior. Role-play the difference between a whiny voice and his normal voice, or suggest, "You're welcome to bring your toys into the breakfast nook or help me prepare the meal if you'd like to be nearby."

3. Follow through. It's vital that you *completely* ignore your child's undue requests for attention—even a simple "Remember what

we talked about?" is attention, and a payoff. Walk away, or engage in another activity.

As you ignore demands for Undue Attention, it's essential that you are employing Mind, Body & Soul Time to provide your child plenty of positive attention. If you don't, the misbehaviors are unlikely to disappear, and you might find yourself facing some new challenges.

When to Use It

- When you've determined that your child is pursuing the mistaken goal of Undue Attention
- When your child repeatedly pesters you for attention, even if it's negative
- Only in concert with Mind, Body & Soul Time and other positive tools
- Only after you've revealed in advance what you're going to do

Why It Works

With the mistaken goal of Undue Attention, your child is seeking any kind of attention from you—he's accepted the fact that it might be negative. Every time you acknowledge the misbehavior, even with a brief admonishment like "Use your big-boy voice," you give your child the payoff, or reward, he's looking for, guaranteeing it will happen again.

The only way to effectively counteract these types of misbehaviors as they're happening is to ignore them, since anything else you do involves giving your child the payoff he wants.

However, this tool will be effective long-term only if it's used along with Mind, Body & Soul Time and other tools that will build up a positive sense of belonging and significance in your child. Every child needs these emotional goals to be met, and will try to get them met one way or another. Your goal is to make sure these needs are filled in positive ways.

Once your child sees that you're not going to respond to his attention-seeking misbehaviors, and he's getting his need for a sense of belonging met in a positive way, he'll no longer harbor a mistaken belief that he needs to badger, whine or act helpless to achieve his goal.

Tips for Success

- It's essential that you reveal in advance what you're going to do (or not going to do). Otherwise, this tool can feel like punishment. Make sure you choose a calm moment to talk to your child about his misbehavior.
- If your child relentlessly follows you after you've ignored his misbehavior, continue to ignore him. The moment you give in, you'll send your child the message that you can be worn down if he keeps at it long enough. Don't be discouraged if the situation escalates into a tantrum. You'll learn how to deal with that in the next section.
- Mind, Body & Soul Time is your best friend! Be committed to your time with your child, twice a day for ten minutes each time. Remember, if we ignore negative attention-seeking behaviors, we have to provide plenty of positive reinforcement so her attention basket is full.
- Take Time for Training is a great tool for helping your child learn what constitutes a necessary interruption, or to completely train your child in the tasks he most commonly asks for help with. You know he can do them, so make sure he does, too.

- Use Encouragement throughout the day to continually foster a sense of belonging and significance.

Attention Overload

The Tool Explained

Being proactive about providing positive attention to your child is the most effective way to address the mistaken goal of Undue Attention long term. This is best done with regular Mind, Body & Soul Time. However, there may be times—for instance, when company is coming or you have a conference call—when you really need your child to cooperate, and won't be able to as effectively manage misbehavior as it's happening.

That's when Attention Overload comes in handy. With this tool, you fill your child's attention basket just before the doorbell or phone is supposed to ring, so that your child is much less likely to resort to negative means to get the attention he needs.

The process is simple: Plan on Mind, Body & Soul Time for ten to fifteen minutes immediately preceding your commitment. You'll need to schedule it in, which isn't always easy if you're putting the finishing touches on dinner or compiling notes, but the benefits of having a well-mannered child when you are most counting on her good behavior will outweigh the investment.

When to Use It

- When you have an important commitment that's ripe for interruptions from a child seeking attention
- Just before your commitment is planned—if you use Atten-

tion Overload too far in advance, the effectiveness will be reduced

Why It Works

When you're visiting with other adults, preparing a complex meal or slogging through your taxes, your child knows she doesn't have your attention, but still needs to feel a sense of belonging, particularly if the situation is also stressful for her (she's probably not enjoying the fact that your boss is over for dinner, for instance). What's more, because of the nature of these types of occurrences, you may not have the capacity to nip behavior problems in the bud using Choices or Encouragement, as you normally would.

This tool helps you proactively prepare your child as best you can, and set her up for success. When her need for a sense of belonging is met in advance, she'll be less likely to seek it in negative ways.

Tips for Success

- If you have multiple children, start with the one most likely to behave appropriately when you use Attention Overload. End with the one most likely to demand undue attention.
- Consider sharing Attention Overload duties with your spouse, if possible.

Owen Revisited

Paul has read this chapter, and he's ready to address Owen's Undue Attention misbehavior. Here's what his morning might now look like.

TODAY, Owen is headed off to preschool. Once Owen is washed and dressed, Paul makes the usual announcement: "Hey, buddy, it's time for our Owen and Daddy Time! We have ten minutes, what would you like to do?"

Owen runs for his Play-Doh—his favorite activity nowadays has been sculpting zoo animals and allowing them to smash one another. Paul lets Owen set a timer and starts forming a blue giraffe, a particularly fun creature to smash.

When the timer rings, Paul and Owen race each other to gather their things for the day before having breakfast, following their morning When-Then Routine. An avid timekeeper, Paul has allowed enough time to eat and get out the door, but of course dawdling can slow even the most perfect plan.

As if on cue, Owen fiddles with his shoelaces. "Can you tie my shoes, Daddy?" he asks Paul.

Having revealed in advance that he'll be ignoring requests for help he knows his son doesn't need, Paul remains in the kitchen, clearing up dishes and gathering up paperwork to drop off at the office.

Owen comes into the kitchen, shoes untied. "Tie my shoes, Daddy!" he demands.

Paul leaves the room, knowing his son will follow him. Completely unfazed, he picks up his bag, puts on a jacket and walks out to the car. He pulls the garbage can out to the curb, puts his things into the passenger seat and opens Owen's car door. Then he heads back to the house. As if by magic, Owen has put his shoes on and tied them.

"All right, Owen, time to leave! Do you want to listen to a CD in the car, or read your book?" Paul asks, to keep the momentum going.

"A CD!" Owen says, heading out the door.

"You got it!" agrees Paul, knowing Owen has a stash of CDs that are kept in the car.

Pulling out of the driveway, Owen panics: "I forgot Dino!"

"Sorry, kiddo, but we took time to gather up our things before breakfast. We'll see him when we get home." Fortunately, Paul has also revealed this Natural Consequence in advance, so although Owen whines, there's nothing to be done.

That afternoon, as usual, Owen plays under the care of a watchful nanny and Paul works in his home office. However, the nanny receives an urgent phone call and has to leave early, unexpectedly. This would be no big deal, except Paul is scheduled to be on an important conference call half an hour later—and his clients certainly won't understand a 4-year-old whining for a story. Paul decides to spend fifteen minutes just before the call begins filling Owen's attention basket using Attention Overload. Then he talks to Owen about the fact that he will ignore any requests for Undue Attention: "Owen, I need to be on the phone for a little while. If you interrupt, I won't respond—I'll be focused on my call." Then he helps Owen find a few of his favorite toys he can play with quietly nearby.

Miraculously, Paul survives the call with only one quick interruption, which he successfully ignores. It helps that he and Owen have been working on phone manners and training Owen for what constitutes a necessary interruption. Afterward, Paul encourages Owen: "Thanks for being so patient while I was on the phone— I was able to really focus and get a lot of work done!"

Owen still occasionally asks for Paul's attention when he can't give it, but the repeated badgering has disappeared. Both are much happier for it.

THE mistaken goal of Undue Attention is a clue that your child doesn't feel as though she's receiving the positive attention she needs. Yes, she's misbehaving, but as you work to train her in the proper behavior, you'll need to make sure you foster her sense of belonging. Neglecting to address Undue Attention or addressing it in the wrong way—such as omitting Mind, Body & Soul Time and other tools that provide a sense of belonging and significance— will leave your child unfulfilled as a member of your family, and she's likely to progress to the next mistaken goal, Power.

Mini-Tool: Avoid Special Service

One common type of Undue Attention is called "Special Service," and it happens when your child consistently demands you do something for her that you know she can do perfectly well herself. Whether this comes in the form of solving a simple math problem or spreading jam on toast, it's a misbehavior—and it needs to stop.

With Special Service, our kids are unknowingly either seeking our attention by trying to keep us busy with them, or trying to exert power and manipulate us. And this isn't just a simple "Can I have a bowl of cereal?" from a 4-year-old who might not be able to reach the box (although you can address that, too, with Control the Environment). If you're irritated because you know the child is perfectly capable yet consistently expects your help, it's Special Service.

And although you might be tempted to zip your child's hoodie for him so you can get out the door on time, it's important to avoid Special Service for your child's sake. By withholding your help in these situations, you reinforce the fact that you have faith in your child's capabilities, and you avoid allowing him to manipulate you to get his way.

Here's what to say (in your calmest voice) next time your child is demanding Special Service:

"Actually, I'm going to let you handle that, because I know you can do it."

Or: "You're really growing up, and I have confidence that you can do it."

After you deliver the message that you won't be helping, simply walk away so you don't have to listen to whining, nagging or badgering. Your kids will soon get the point and develop a healthier sense of independence.

Mistaken Goal #2: Power

Madison used to be such a sweet child. Sure, she's always been spunky and has never been afraid to speak her mind, but mother and daughter have generally gotten along well.

Lately, though, Rebecca has been wondering if the terrible teens have set in early. Although Madison is only ten years old, she's been challenging everything Rebecca asks of her.

"Time to pack for your Girl Scout hike," Rebecca orders. "You'll need a snack, water, your compass and your field guide. You should also probably bring some extra socks since it's been so wet. Come on, hop to it!"

She's met with an angry "Whatever. I can get what I need, I'm not a baby!" as Madison storms out of the room.

Another time, Rebecca directs Madison to give up the TV remote, as her TV time is over for the day.

"No, I'm not done with my show!" Madison yells for the whole house to hear. She follows up her exclamation by sitting on the remote.

And forget trying to get Madison to help out. "Madison, I need you to fold the laundry. And don't fold the towels so unevenly this time, they were really sloppy when you did it that way last time," Rebecca commands.

This garners the response "Why do I have to do it? Jason never helps out around here!" And any repeated plea for help is only ignored.

Rebecca hates to argue, but finds herself battling back every time, and even using physical force to pry the TV remote from her daughter's hands. But the situation only escalates, and usually doesn't end until feelings are hurt and doors are slammed.

Madison used to be such a sweet child, but now she's gone sour. And Rebecca's left wondering if she'll ever enjoy her daughter again.

As I'm sure you've guessed, Madison is a prime example of a child with a mistaken belief that she can gain a healthy sense of power and significance by initiating power struggles. This mistaken goal is called Power, and it's characterized by tantrums, back-talking, eye-rolling, ignoring and doing the opposite of what parents ask.

Madison is likely seeking negative power because she may not be receiving enough positive power through other means. It could be that she's entering a new phase of independence and needs some additional power to make her own decisions. And Rebecca certainly isn't helping the situation with all her ordering, directing and correcting in the way she bosses Madison around. In fact, too much use of the Parent Ego State is likely to exasperate anyone and will almost always lead to Power-seeking behaviors. Nevertheless, Madison's actions are clear misbehaviors, and need to be corrected.

These types of negative actions are likely due to the mistaken goal of Power if they:

1. Are common, and repeated
2. Leave you feeling angry, provoked or challenged
3. Escalate when you reprimand, with the child raising his voice and continuing the battle

Power-seeking behaviors are a sign that your child's need for a sense of significance isn't being met in some key way. You may be spending too much time in the Parent Ego State, ordering, directing and correcting everything he does and stripping him of a sense of independence. Or it could be that he's ready to make more of his own decisions, but you haven't recognized his heightened level of maturity yet (possibly because your 5-year-old seems to be acting like a 2-year-old with his childish tantrums). Whatever the root of the issue is, there are lots of things you can do to help.

As the misbehavior is happening, you need to remove the Power "fix" your child would normally receive from it. To address back talk and tantrums, walk away, and refuse to participate by arguing, negotiating, explaining or even listening. If you get involved, you only reinforce your child's misguided attempts to find a sense of power. For other power struggles, defuse them with tools like Either-Or, When-Then, Consequences and Routines. A few new tools we'll talk about next, including Invite Cooperation, Withdraw from Conflict, and Using "I Feel" Statements, will give you some additional strategies.

To address this mistaken goal long term, the most important thing you can do is foster a strong sense of significance through empowering tools like Take Time for Training, Encouragement and Choices. Limit your time spent in the Parent Ego State, and relinquish some control to your child. Just as with Undue Attention, if you don't work to correct the underlying issue of the mistaken goal in the right way, your short-term fixes will fail, and your child could progress to the next mistaken goal, Revenge.

As a final note, many parents work to solve Power-seeking misbehaviors by using punishment. We've already talked a lot about why punishment is ineffective, but I want to stress here that it can be extremely detrimental. If you punish Power-seeking misbehavior, you're setting yourself and your child up to make the problem worse. It'll quickly turn into the vicious cycle characteristic of the tough cases of Revenge, which we'll cover in a later section.

Invite Cooperation

The Tool Explained

Inviting Cooperation is a way to be proactive about avoiding power struggles with your kids. With this tool, you adapt your tone of voice and the words you choose to be respectful rather than demanding. Instead of bossing your child around, say things like "Anything you can do to help clean up the kitchen would be much appreciated," or "What's your plan for getting your project done?" Both of these allow your child to complete a task in a meaningful way, but also save face and not feel like he's being ordered around. They empower your child to help out on his terms, but still get the job done. Other phrases you could try:

"We need to unload the camping equipment before dinner. Anything you can do to help would be fabulous!"

"Dad looks really tired from doing all the yardwork. I'm sure he'd appreciate a second set of hands."

"I'm feeling overwhelmed with getting everything done before our company arrives. Anything you can do to get your brothers dressed and looking presentable would be a huge help."

"Saturday is garage clean-out day. Anything you guys could do to pitch in would get the job done a lot faster!"

Consider what you're asking of your child. Prioritize your requests—no one likes to be treated like a household slave. If you're asking for too many insignificant things you could easily do yourself ("Bring me my glass of iced tea—I don't want to get off the couch," or "Can you run upstairs and get my glasses?"), you're less likely to get cooperation in the bigger tasks. Make sure that the contributions you ask your child to make are meaningful to him and to you, and encourage his help and hard work.

And it's okay to be direct in instructing your kids at times, such as saying, "It's time to leave for school—I need you to put your shoes on now." But not all of our communication should be directing and bossing our kids around. If we work to minimize directing and increase "inviting," we'll be much more successful in getting our kids to cooperate.

When to Use It

- Anytime you're asking your child to complete a task or adopt a certain behavior
- Especially in situations that would normally produce a power struggle

Why It Works

The Invite Cooperation tool works because it falls directly in line with the Empowerment Paradigm. We can't control another person, but we can control ourselves—and the words we use, the way we speak to our kids and the things we ask them to do.

When we Invite Cooperation, we limit the ordering, directing and correcting we do in the Parent Ego State, and instead operate in the Adult Ego State to get our kids on board with a plan. This shift in tone of voice and word choice can mean the difference between a "Sure, Mom" and a "But I don't *want* to!" Remember, the

Adult Ego State is known for inviting cooperation, while the Parent Ego State is characterized by brewing power struggles.

Using carefully chosen words (not to mention carefully chosen tasks), we let our kids know that we respect them and their time. They'll come to understand that while we don't think of them as personal servants, we do ask that they be responsible for helping with the house and fulfilling their own obligations, and we are grateful for their meaningful contributions.

All of these factors working together will help you get the response you're looking for—or at least limit the talking back or negotiating that kids are prone to.

Tips for Success

- If you're used to ordering your kids around a lot, it's okay to start slow. Practice this tool (even take some time to think out a phrase in advance) and soon you'll be more comfortable with finding agreeable phrases and delivering them in the Adult Ego State.
- It's likely you have already put this strategy into practice with your coworkers—most of the time, you wouldn't boss them around and expect them to blindly follow you. So if you're stumped, pretend you're at work and need to get someone on board with a task.
- Even with regular use of this tool, you'll still likely meet with some occasional resistance. If you do, follow up with a When-Then or other appropriate tool.

Withdraw from Conflict

The Tool Explained

Counteracting Power-seeking misbehaviors as they're happening requires you to completely remove the payoff your children would receive if you argued, battled or negotiated with them. That means you'll need to withdraw entirely from the situation.

To begin using this tool, first reveal in advance that you won't be responding to your child's negative behaviors. Be specific, and say something like "I expect us to speak to each other with a calm and respectful tone. When you talk back to me, I'm not going to respond—I'm going to just walk away. When you're able to speak calmly and respectfully, I'm here for you."

When you recognize the Power-seeking misbehavior on your child's part (which you'll know because you feel angry or provoked), simply disengage—involve yourself in another activity or leave the room, retreating to your bedroom if you need to.

Your child may have a full-blown meltdown the first couple of times you use this tool. If that happens, simply ignore it. Your child has the right to throw a fit, but as long as she's in a safe place, you don't need to pay any attention—the tool will lose its effectiveness if you do.

Some parents question whether this strategy is cruel or rude. Take heart that you are withdrawing from the behavior, not from the child. When she's calmed down and can be respectful, be prepared to speak to her about the incident in a calm, relaxed fashion. If necessary, you can train your child in the correct behavior at a neutral time.

When to Use It

- To counteract repeated negative Power-seeking misbehaviors
- Only along with empowering tools such as Mind, Body & Soul Time, Choices, Encouragement and When-Then Routines
- Only after you've revealed in advance that you're going to ignore your children's attempts to create conflict, and will be happy to talk to them again when they can do so calmly

Why It Works

When you use the Withdraw from Conflict tool, you're sending the message to your child that you refuse to engage in your child's misbehavior. You remove the "power trip" she'd normally receive by battling it out with you, which is the payoff she's looking for. If you remain consistent, you will notice a decrease in Power-seeking misbehaviors.

This tool works only if you use it in conjunction with some of the more empowering tools, such as Take Time for Training, Routines and Choices. If you don't proactively replace the negative power with positive power, you and your child will continue to suffer and the problem could worsen into one of Revenge.

Tips for Success

- Be consistent and follow through. You must remove the payoff entirely, every time your child exhibits a negative Power-seeking misbehavior. If you eventually give in, it teaches your child that he just has to go longer and possibly louder, and he'll eventually get the best of you.
- Young children in particular may follow you from room to room, or even cling to you, as you do your best to withdraw. In this

situation, I recommend making use of the Bathroom Technique. Simply retreat to an area of the house that's usually associated with privacy, such as the bathroom. Tell your child, "When I hear your Calm Voice, I'll come out and we can talk." Then close and lock the door. Sit tight until your child calms down (it will happen, I promise). And don't worry—you won't have to use this technique more than a couple of times, at the most.

- When you address your child after the incident, be sure to use your Calm Voice and remain in the Adult Ego State.
- Proactively use tools like Take Time for Training, Encouragement and Choices for long-term success. Make sure you're empowering your child regularly throughout the day, and avoiding telling your child what to do and how to do it all the time.

TOOLBOX SOLUTION #17

Using "I Feel" Statements

The Tool Explained

In every difficult situation, communication plays a huge role in defusing—or fueling—angry and hurt feelings. For instance, during a misbehavior our first impulse might be to say something like "You always leave your stuff all over the living room!" or "You never remember to put your dishes in the sink!" Beginning a statement with "you always" or "you never," however, only puts the other person on the defensive, and often compels them to be less receptive to your point of view.

Using "I Feel" Statements, you'll instead begin a respectful conversation that can be used to solve the underlying problem.

An "I Feel" statement has three parts:

1. I feel . . . (hurt, angry, annoyed, disrespected)
2. When you . . . (throw my . . . , forget to . . .)
3. I wish . . . (you would be more careful . . . , you wouldn't take my . . .)

So, instead of saying, "You always forget to take off your shoes in the house!" you would say, "I feel upset when you wear your shoes in the house because it tracks mud everywhere and I'm left to clean it up. I wish you would take them off as soon as you come inside." In another situation, instead of exploding with "Can't you ever think to put your dishes in the dishwasher?!" you could tell your child, "I feel disrespected when you leave your dishes all over the sink, expecting me to clean them up. I would really appreciate it if you would put your own dishes and cups into the dishwasher when you're done with them." No one can argue with your feelings, and your child now has a respectful statement to respond to—she's not being directly accused or "put in her place." You can invite her to share her feelings, and work out an agreement using a conversation instead of a shouting match.

Use this tool to defuse power struggles and hurtful situations, whether you're addressing your children or your spouse. In fact, this is an excellent tool to model with your spouse—not only is it empowering for both of you, but you'll set a positive example for your kids.

As you teach your children to use this tool, role-playing will help them practice. In fact, this is one that everyone will probably need to practice—and you can expect it to take some time to integrate "I Feel" Statements into your everyday communications.

When to Use It

- To communicate clearly during high-stress situations
- To work through and defuse power struggles
- To calmly discuss misbehaviors with your child

Why It Works

"I Feel" Statements help both parents and children communicate their feelings without putting either on the defensive. When you put the emphasis on what you're feeling, rather than what the other person is doing, you can express what you need to say without finger-pointing, criticizing or attacking.

These statements are especially important to use with kids because they teach children how to identify feelings and label them. With this knowledge, they can better understand their own emotions in explosive situations and eventually learn to temper their reactions.

What's more, they reinforce the idea that feelings are okay. Some actions aren't (for instance, throwing things when you're angry), but it's perfectly natural and acceptable to feel hurt, upset and sad at times.

Finally, "I Feel" Statements teach kids to empathize with others, developing their emotional intelligence. All of these factors will work in the long term to help your whole family resolve conflicts with greater understanding and acceptance.

Tips for Success

- Practice! "I Feel" Statements may seem awkward at first, but with time you'll be able to use them with plenty of success.
- Avoid turning a respectful "I Feel" Statement into criticism. For

instance, "I feel mad when you're such a pig and eat all the cookies before anyone else has a chance. I wish you would go on a diet and quit eating us out of house and home" is hardly a helpful statement.

- Use "I Feel" Statements only with your Calm Voice, and in the Adult Ego State.

Madison Revisited

Let's go back to Madison and her mom. Rebecca is tired of struggling for power with her daughter, and decides to implement strategies to counteract Power-seeking misbehaviors, including changing her own behavior. Here's how their story continues:

ONE Thursday evening after dinner, Rebecca has a brief conversation with her daughter. "Honey, do you have a few minutes to chat? I want you to know how much I love you. I've also been wanting to let you know that I feel disrespected when you talk back to me or speak to me with a negative tone. From now on, I'm not going to respond to your back talk or disrespectful comments to me," she says. "Instead, I'm going to ignore them and walk away. I love you very much and I'm always happy to talk with you about anything, but only when you can speak calmly and nicely to me."

As she expects, Madison responds only with a "Whatever. I *am* nice to you," which Rebecca ignores.

Rebecca gets her first opportunity to truly put the tools she's learned into action the next morning, when asking Madison to straighten up her room.

Rebecca begins by inviting cooperation: "Madison, anything you could do to tidy up your room would be much appreciated."

"It's *my* room, what do you care what it looks like!" counters Madison in her haughtiest tone.

Normally, Rebecca would have snapped back, "While you live in *my* house, you'll do what you're told, young lady!" but she refrains. Instead, she delivers a When-Then—"*When* you've straightened your room, *then* you will be allowed your technology time for the day"—and heads downstairs to the laundry room, where the sound of the dryer helps drown out Madison's "It's not fair! *None* of my friends have to clean their rooms, *ever!*"

After twenty minutes of pouting and ten minutes of actual work, Madison appears downstairs and turns on the computer. Rebecca can't resist sneaking a peek into her daughter's room and sees that it has, indeed, miraculously, been straightened.

That afternoon, Rebecca implements another part of her plan: letting her little girl accept some responsibility, and make some empowering decisions. While they're out running errands, Rebecca suggests stopping at the grocery store.

"I think you're old enough to start planning some of the family meals," she says. "Why don't you choose a meal that you'd like us to have for supper, and then you can help me buy the ingredients we need to make it? What should we have?"

Madison is surprised at the suggestion, but soon becomes engrossed in deciding between two of her favorites: tacos and veggie pizza. At the store, she learns about picking the freshest vegetables and checking prices, and at home that night she learns how to brown meat (she chose tacos), warm tortillas and safely chop tomatoes and onions. The training is a great success—Madison begins talking about what she wants to make next week, and the whole family has enjoyed the meal.

Rebecca then encourages Madison, telling her, "You really made a huge difference in my day by making dinner—thank you for your hard work!" She continues to find meaningful opportunities for Madison to make choices and contribute to the family, encouraging all her efforts.

But they're not out of the woods yet. Madison isn't going to give up quite so easily the fights that she's come to almost enjoy. The next confrontation is a big one. It begins with Rebecca telling Madison she can't rent a PG-13 movie for her upcoming slumber party.

"But *everyone* watches PG-13 movies, I'm the only one who's not allowed to watch them!" whines Madison.

Rebecca walks away.

Madison escalates the challenge. "This slumber party is going to suck if we have to watch a kid movie! You must hate me! I hate *you!*"

Rebecca doesn't respond.

"If you're worried about bad words, I already know them!" And Madison lets out a string of profanity, upping the stakes even more. She's sure to get her mom's attention this way.

Rebecca continues to ignore her.

Finally, with no one to fuel her on, Madison loses steam. She goes to her room to sulk.

A little while later, Madison is headed outside to play with her brothers.

"Are we still going to the movie store?" she asks her mom.

"Sure. I'll be ready to leave in about twenty minutes," Rebecca answers calmly.

The two make it through the store with only a little whining on Madison's part, and leave with a PG movie that doesn't suck at all.

Things are much better for Rebecca and Madison. Rebecca continues to empower Madison with Encouragement, Choices and Training, and makes sure she's spending Mind, Body & Soul Time with her, too. Not that Madison never fights back, but the struggles aren't so bitter and Rebecca has the tools she needs to empower and train Madison even through her misbehavior.

Mistaken Goal #3: Revenge

Colby's parents don't know whether to be angry or hurt. They love their son, but he's never been more difficult to manage in his ten years of life. Not only is he acting up all the time, he seems to be personally out to get them.

Admittedly, many of their confrontations nowadays are angry.

"Mom, could you drive me over to Brendan's house?" Colby asks one Saturday morning in March.

"Can't you see I'm busy?" Mom mumbles as she stares at one tax form after another.

"Please? He only lives ten minutes away!"

"I said *no*, don't you ever listen?" yells Mom, doubly aggravated by the fact that she can't find the receipt for the new printer she bought for her home office in the last year.

"How about tonight? His parents said I could stay over," tries Colby.

"Colby, I'm going shopping with your aunt Stephanie this

afternoon, and then the Hendersons are coming over for dinner. I just don't have time to drive you. Now would you quit asking questions so I can get these taxes done?!"

Colby explodes: "I don't *care* about your #*$@& taxes, I just want to go to Brendan's house!" he rants—and then in an unprecedented move, he swipes at a stack of his mom's tax documents and sends them swirling off the table.

Another time, Colby's been asked to rake the leaves. It's not his favorite thing to do, but he doesn't mind the task—he likes being outside, and of course jumping in the pile when he's finished. After working for a good twenty minutes, he's built up a pretty big pile in the front yard, and decides to take a break before doing the backyard. One good jump sends some of the leaves flying. Unfortunately, Dad chose that minute to pull into the driveway, home from work.

"Colby, what are you doing!? You're supposed to rake them up, not scatter them across the yard. Now I'm going to have to finish it," Dad complains.

"I'll *do* it, I'm just taking a break!" insists Colby.

"Well, you didn't do a very good job. You missed all the leaves under the bushes. And at this rate, you won't even be done before dark."

"I'll do it how I want to, you can't boss me around!" shouts Colby.

"Don't talk to me like that, young man!"

"I'll say what I want to!"

The fight escalates, with Dad trying to grab the rake out of Colby's hands, insisting, "You're not even holding it right!"

Finally, Colby tears off on a rampage through his neatly raked leaf pile, sending leaves flying, before dragging the rake's metal tines across the side of his dad's car and throwing it to the ground.

"You rotten kid! I'll make you pay for that!" Dad storms, all the while asking himself what happened to the days when they'd play catch in the yard after work.

But the final straw (lately, anyway) comes when Colby's mom trips over a baseball mitt for the umpteenth time. "Pick up all your sports stuff, it's a huge mess!" she demands.

"No, you can't tell me what to do," retorts Colby.

"I told you to pick it up! Do what I say or you won't like what happens when your dad gets home," Colby's mom warns.

Colby knows exactly what's going to happen when his dad gets home: a big yelling match and maybe a spanking. Nevertheless, he realizes he already has it coming from the fact that he tracked mud all over the kitchen floor earlier in the day.

"He can't hurt me! And neither can you!" Colby runs out of the room as his mom follows.

"Clean up your mess!" she yells. "Or no dessert tonight, or the rest of the week," she adds.

"*You* clean up *your* mess! I hate you and I hate this *@!*# house!" Colby screams back, knocking a stack of dishes onto the floor from the counter. Many of them shatter. Mom heads out after him. Her words say: "You've done it now, young man! I'm taking away your iPod and you're not going out with your friends for two weeks!" But deep down she's thinking, *How did we ever get to this point?*

OVER the years, Colby has tried to gain a sense of belonging and significance any way he can, until finally concluding with a mistaken belief, at ten years old, that he can't achieve them in a positive way. All of his efforts are simply met with more and more punishment. He's been damaged on an emotional level, and feels unlikable and unlovable. Now he's moved on—he's no longer trying to get his parents' attention or prove who's boss. Instead, he's set to get revenge, and to pay his parents back for how they've hurt him.

Colby's parents are equally frustrated. They don't know where they've gone wrong. It doesn't matter how much they punish him, his behavior doesn't change—in fact, it gets worse year by year, month by month. They're at their wit's end, and have even started to wonder if military school would be a good option for Colby.

COLBY has progressed past Undue Attention and Power, and on to the mistaken goal of Revenge. Revenge is characterized by behaviors that are meant to cause physical or emotional harm. When kids act out with Revenge, a parent's natural emotional reaction is hurt and disbelief: "How could my child have done this?" Then anger usually sets in and the child is punished for the act. The punishment reinforces the idea that he is not likable or lovable, which encourages the child to act out again—usually upping the intensity with each subsequent misbehavior.

As we've seen, Colby's parents have been addressing his misbehaviors by using punishment—and that's a big part of the problem. With punishment, a vicious cycle is created. The punishment itself strips a child of positive feelings of belonging and significance, spurring more negative behaviors, and then more punishment.

Remember that all behavior has a purpose, and even an act of Revenge is trying to tell you something. Through a mistaken goal of Revenge, the child is crying out to belong, be understood and feel significant. His actions are saying, "I'm hurting, but you can't even see that. My words say 'I hate you,' but deep down I just want to belong and feel significant in this family."

Breaking the cycle of Revenge means putting an end to the

payoff your child receives from the misbehavior, and stopping the punishment entirely. As the misbehavior is happening, whether your child is unleashing a string of defamatory remarks or sending your laptop crashing to the floor, you need to show the opposite response to what comes naturally, and what your child expects. If you show you feel hurt and come completely unglued, that's when she knows she's been successful in hurting you.

Because your child *wants* to hurt you, you need to pretend that the misbehavior doesn't affect you, and remove the payoff she's looking for. By showing no anger, frustration or dismay, you can send the message that "no laptop is more important than my child. I'm more concerned about why she feels this way." When you and your child have calmed down, tell her, "For you to throw my laptop on the floor, you must really be hurting inside, and I'm sure I'm the reason for much of that. I love you so much. Please help me understand what you're feeling, so I can help."

Most important, don't retaliate with punishment. It may be your natural response, but your number-one priority should instead be to help the child recover from his very real emotional pain. Punishment only reinforces the mistaken belief of "I don't belong" or "I'm not significant," leading to an even more extreme response next time.

With Revenge situations, you'll need to focus on healing and the tools we learned first: Mind, Body & Soul Time, Calm Voice and Encouragement. These will begin the process of helping your child feel loved and empowered. Use them regularly as you work on restoring the relationship. Remember that your child is damaged and will need time to heal, but healing can, and will, happen. If you need to use consequences, stick to Natural Consequences. Logical

Consequences should be avoided as they require parental involvement and will likely feel like punishment to your child.

It's also very important to keep lines of communication open and positive by using "I Feel" Statements. Be sure to look inside yourself to identify how your behaviors and attitudes are fueling the problem. And as you listen to your child, try to see the situation from her perspective. When a relationship becomes this damaged, however, it's often because neither person feels like they can effectively communicate with the other. If you can't talk with your child without using blame or criticism, or if your child simply won't open up to you, it's wise to employ professional help. Even a few counseling sessions can make a big difference in restoring a positive relationship with your child.

If Revenge is left unaddressed, or if it continues to be met with punishment, your child may lapse into Assumed Inadequacy—the fourth mistaken goal.

Mistaken Goal #4: Assumed Inadequacy

Every day when 13-year-old Charlotte returns home from school, she slinks into her room. Occasionally, she comes out to grab a quick snack or use the bathroom, but she mostly just wants to be alone. Her parents don't know what she's doing in there, but it's clear she isn't interested in spending time with the family.

Sometimes Charlotte's parents worry—neither Mom nor Dad can seem to get through to the girl, and in the meantime, her skirts seem to be getting shorter, her grades worse and her mood more sullen. They're not too sure about her new boyfriend, either.

But she's so offended by everything they say that they've all but given up on trying to keep her from going off the deep end. So instead, they just chalk her behavior up to the fact that she's a teenager—she'll come around in a few years, they tell themselves. They'll concentrate on her little brother instead.

However, Charlotte's always required to come out of her room for dinner. Today, she picks at her pork chop, and manages just a few bites of her baked potato. She's not hungry, and wants to go back to her room. After all, the only dinner conversation is a fight between her parents and her brother—he's brought home another C, which has never been good enough. She knows that if she stays at the table much longer, her parents will start in on her—complaining about grades, her new boyfriend or how they think her skirt is too short. They never have anything positive to say.

Charlotte can't wait until she can move out—she still has five years to go until she turns eighteen, and she's already counting the days. Her parents just don't understand her. She doesn't fit in at home and doesn't see the point of trying to have a good relationship with her family. After all, the more time she spends with them, the more she gets yelled at. Good thing she has her friends and her boyfriend to count on—they're the ones who really "get" her.

"Can I be excused?" Charlotte asks quietly.

"Finish your dinner," her dad replies, glancing at his daughter's plate instead of her face. He's tired of dealing with his kids' problems and wishes they'd both just straighten up.

"I'm not hungry," she explains.

"I told you to finish your dinner!" Dad roars.

Charlotte manages a few more bites, and then does her best to hide the uneaten parts of her pork chop under her baked potato skin. By now, the rest of the family is finished so she puts her plate on the counter and heads back to her room.

Unfortunately for her, Charlotte's dad notices the half-eaten pork chop.

"Young lady, we do not waste food in this house! Finish your pork chop *now*, and by the way, you're not going to that slumber party on Friday!" Dad wants to make sure Charlotte learns her lesson—under his roof, you do things his way. And there's no getting through to this girl without being firm.

Charlotte chokes back a retort and cowers to the table with her pork chop. She knows there's no use in arguing. She spends the rest of the night in her room.

THE FOURTH and final mistaken goal of misbehavior is Assumed Inadequacy. At this point, the child has given up. His mistaken belief is that there's nothing he can do to succeed, let alone achieve a sense of belonging and significance. He wants to protect what little self-esteem he has left by completely withdrawing and refusing to try anymore.

There are two types of Assumed Inadequacy. Charlotte is an example of Overall Inadequacy—she's given up on home life entirely and is avoiding her parents as much as possible. The other type is Specific Inadequacy, which is characterized by a child giving up in a subject at school, sports, music or another specific pursuit. In this case, a child might use phrases like "School is dumb," or "I hate sports," and make no effort. In both cases, the child's feeling is the same: "I'll never be successful, so why even try?"

Overall Inadequacy usually develops after a child's Revenge behavior is consistently addressed with punishment, or when the child is allowed to continue in his misbehavior. The child is extremely discouraged, and each episode of punishment only digs a deeper hole, convincing him that he'll never belong, or feel significant. With Specific Inadequacy, the child feels increasingly discouraged by his inability to succeed, by pressure from parents and from punishment that may accompany his failures. As a result, he feels he'll never be successful. In both cases, the child sees no point in making any effort anymore and only wants to be left alone. Essentially, he's given up and checked out.

Naturally, this leaves parents feeling equally discouraged, and at the point of giving up themselves. This is the last thing we want to do. If we give up on our child, he'll only give up further.

But while Assumed Inadequacy may seem like a hopeless situation, there are things you can do to renew your child's feelings of belonging and significance, and empower your child.

First and foremost, stop all punishment, for the reasons we've discussed before. And especially in the case of Specific Inadequacy, make sure you're not putting any undue pressure on your child to perform, as many high-achieving parents are prone to do. Begin instead to encourage every effort in the right direction, whether your child is facing Overall or Specific Inadequacy. For instance, if your 6-year-old has completely given up on learning to read, you could encourage him for simply picking up a book and looking at the pictures. Ask him, "Which pictures are your favorite? Should we try to find out what the characters are doing?"

Be sure to respond to your child in a loving way—remember that he's very deeply discouraged. Regular Mind, Body & Soul Time will work wonders, as will regular use of a Calm Voice, Encouragement, Take Time for Training and other empowering tools. Avoid using Logical Consequences, though—in your child's damaged state, he'll see them as punishment.

You'll also want to consider using some outside resources to help diagnose or counsel a problem. If your child has a diagnosed learning difference, hiring a tutor or getting him special help at school will aid your efforts. And in the case of Overall Inadequacy, family counseling sessions would probably do everyone some good. Remember that your child's emotional health and ultimate success are at stake, and it's your responsibility as a parent to guide your child in the right direction using whatever resources you have available.

Some parents have difficulty determining whether their child is suffering from Undue Attention (as one of the characteristics is acting helpless) or Assumed Inadequacy. To decide, evaluate your own reaction and your child's. If you're simply irritated or annoyed, rather than extremely discouraged, it's probably a case of Undue Attention. And if your child seeks your help or attention, rather than hide his math scores and hope you don't ask about them, this is another big clue that it's Undue Attention. Either way, you need to address the problem, but your strategies will differ.

Final Words About Mistaken Goals

Childhood is complicated business—and so is parenthood. The beauty of understanding mistaken goals and being able to diagnose them allows you to see misbehavior in a completely different light. Your child's misbehavior is trying to tell you something about how he perceives his sense of belonging and significance. Identifying the mistaken goal allows you to be more strategic in correcting misbehavior, with better results. Instead of responding with your gut reaction—which will likely make the behavior continue and even escalate—you can take a step back, evaluate what is really going on and how you contribute to the problem, and select the appropriate tools from the Toolbox to correct the behavior and address the underlying factors.

Mistaken goals can be harder to diagnose after the age of eleven. At this point, kids are looking to their peer groups for acceptance instead of to their parents. The misbehaviors could appear as thrill-seeking behaviors, promiscuity, drug abuse, sexual behavior and a concern over material possessions. When in doubt, it's always wise to seek professional help in diagnosing or addressing a problem.

No matter your child's age or your family's situation, take heart that you *can* reestablish a healthy relationship between yourself and your troubled child. It will take time, work and lots of love— but your child is always worth it.

SIBLING RIVALRY

Everyone Can *Just Get Along*
(Most of the Time, Anyway)

Little Maria doesn't know it, but she has a pretty cushy life. At just under three years old, she's the apple of her parents' eyes—not to mention her grandparents', who enthusiastically rearrange their busy schedules if she so much as points to a park she'd like to visit or a pony she'd like to ride. She returns the favor: twirling on command, singing the "Puppy Dog Song" and planting kisses left and right.

One day, Maria's parents excitedly sit her down on the couch after dinner. "We love you so much," they tell her. "And we make a pretty good family, don't we? Well, in a few months, we'll have a new person in our family—a new baby!"

When everyone else is smiling, Maria does, too. Accordingly, she cracks a grin, unsure what she's supposed to say, think or sing.

"Won't that be fun?" Maria's parents add. Then they show her a picture of a blob only vaguely resembling a little person, and point out the baby's arms, legs and nose.

Maria still doesn't know what to think, but as long as her parents are happy, she is too. As she enjoys playing with her baby doll and pointing out babies at the grocery store or library, she begins to think that a baby at home might be a really good thing.

And then one day, months later, Maria wakes up in the morning to find Grandma Jo peeking into her room. After the requisite hugs and kisses, and a comment about how snuggly-wuggly she looks in her fluffy poodle jammies, Grandma ecstatically tells Maria that her new baby brother has arrived.

Maria looks around the room and, seeing nothing and starting to wonder where her parents are, gives Grandma a quizzical look.

"We'll go to the hospital to visit Baby and Mommy and Daddy as soon as you're dressed and have had something to eat!"

Maria had been looking forward to "Bubble Day" at preschool that morning, but is curious and fairly excited herself. Grandma fixes chocolate-chip teddy bear pancakes for breakfast, and then leads Maria out to the car.

At the hospital, Maria arrives to find several aunts and uncles already there. Mommy is buried beneath presents and pillows, and a baby—not nearly as cute as the ones Maria's seen in pictures—is in her arms crying. Maria is hurried into the room and plopped onto her daddy's lap for a family picture. Then she's gushed over: "What a wonderful big sister you'll be!" and finally formally introduced to the newborn, who's a little bit bigger than her own baby doll, but a lot heavier and more wiggly. As luck would have it, a little gas bubble escapes Jack's lips as he's eased into Maria's arms, and he seems to smile. Maria decides that she likes him.

Over the next few days and weeks, though, she's not so sure. Maria's first doubts about her baby brother come from the fact that he's constantly, inconceivably, annoyingly loud. But while Maria is scolded for being too noisy in the house if she so much as raises her voice or bangs her toy pots around, Baby Jack is cooed over until he's quiet and happy again. Which lasts all of five minutes.

He's also cooed over every time he poops, doesn't poop, sleeps, wakes up, eats, spits up, frowns and smiles. Maria has pointed out a few times that she can do those things—and much cooler stuff, too—but she's only given a cursory "Very nice, Maria!" when she brings it up.

It seems that everyone has gifts for the baby—he's outfitted in brand-new clothes and entertained with brand-new toys. Some kind souls bring Maria a small toy when they lavish Jack with a fancy new outfit, and most ask her how she's enjoying being a big sister. She just smiles and twirls, vaguely remembering how things used to be.

As Jack grows, he takes possession of many of Maria's old toys and belongings. Not that she really plays with them anymore (she's long outgrown the giraffe rattle and the soft jiggly ball), but she was used to counting them as hers. She's complained, but only received a "Don't be silly, you're far too old for those toys. You have your own toys."

But the worst thing is the fact that Maria is no longer the center of her loved ones' world. Sure, in the first few weeks she got to go out for ice cream with her grandparents or even her daddy a couple of times. But since then, she feels like she could parade a team of elephants through the living room—or even be "good" for an entire day—and no one would notice. Maria misses all the attention. And she begins to really, really, really dislike her baby brother (she's not allowed to use the word *hate*).

Maria starts to comment on her frustrations, but is only reprimanded. "He's not stinky, he's a baby!" they tell her. Or "He *is* fun, isn't he cute?" Or "But you *love* Jack, remember?"

Poor Maria has been dethroned—and she couldn't be more unhappy. She decides that Baby Jack may just be the worst thing that's happened to her in her three years of life.

Why Siblings Make Good Rivals

We see it all the time: The sisters who talk every day even though they live on opposite sides of the country. The brothers who choke up with tears while delivering the best-man speech at each other's wedding. The brother-sister duos who bike across vast expanses of wilderness together to celebrate one or the other graduating from college.

These are the people we dream of our kids becoming. Ever since we brought number 2 home from the hospital, we fantasized about how they'd grow together, play together and stay out of mischief together (as long as we're dreaming). We build them tree houses so they'll have a place to call their own, take them on magical family vacations so they'll forge powerful memories, and make them hug each other anytime one hurts the other's feelings.

And so why does it seem like, no matter what we do, our children would much rather be each other's best enemy than best friend? Why do we hear more bickering than laughing for days on end? Why do *we* cringe at the thought of them sharing a bedroom?

Whether your kids seem to fight all the time, or only engage in the occasional spat, the topic of sibling rivalry is an important one—even only children need to learn the fundamentals of peaceful relationships, communication, problem solving and conflict resolution. This chapter will give you the tools you need to make sure everyone can figure out how to get along.

The unfortunate truth about sibling relationships is that a natural sense of rivalry sets in, not coincidentally, just as the second child is born. There's nothing you can do to prevent it. As you can see in Maria's story above, a newborn in the house can turn an older sibling's life upside down as she now plays second fiddle to a tiny, whiny, stinky little being. And no matter how much you love them both (and each additional child), there's no guarantee they'll love each other a hundred percent of the time, at any age.

Birth order characteristics can play a role in each child's feeling of their place in the family, and one thing's certain: The oldest child *used to be* an only child, receiving all the attention, until the baby entered the house. As in Maria's case, a new addition to the family, unless it's a goldfish or a puppy, is likely to make even the most caring firstborn feel angry, hurt and even betrayed. Once the honeymoon period ends, there are some real problems that can crop up as rivalry takes hold. All of a sudden, family life has become a competition.

According to Adlerian psychology, competition is at the root of sibling rivalry. Any child may compete for his parents' attention the moment he realizes he's lost it—whether Dad is simply catching up with a college buddy on the phone or Mommy is nursing a newborn. While a phone conversation is short-lived, a baby is here to stay, and even the youngest child can figure out that it's not the diaper or bottle demanding attention—it's Little Brother. This initial competition for attention eventually becomes a competition about each child's place in the family as the kids grow older, and finally over possessions. And when there's competition, there's fighting.

But as much as you try to maintain a harmonious family atmosphere, there are also some things we do unknowingly to counteract our own efforts. Once we address these, we can get down to the real business of stopping "all that fighting, for heaven's sake!"

Are You Behind Your Kids' Fights?

Sometimes it doesn't seem to take much for an argument to erupt between our kids. Simply hand one a blue plate and another a red one, and fireworks may ensue. But there are things we can do to decrease the level of competition in our household and reduce the likelihood of fighting. One of the biggies is to make sure we're not comparing our kids through labels, spoken or implied.

We talked about labels a few chapters ago, and how even positive ones can be very discouraging to our kids. Beyond discouragement, they also give rise to and sustain a spirit of competition between siblings, even though we don't mean for them to. They draw comparisons, so if one child is "the musical one," it implies that the other one isn't. Do you think this pair will be cheering each other on at the upcoming piano competition, or instead making faces over the music stand? With labels, no one wins—the labeled child is trapped by it (what happens if the "pretty" sister wakes up with a giant zit?), and her siblings can't measure up (no cute haircut can fix a nose that's seemingly too big). It's a recipe that's ripe for resentment, as we (unintentionally) force our kids to vie for their place in our family, and for belonging and significance within their "roles." Often, the effects continue into adolescence and adulthood.

It's not just the obvious, spoken labels we need to watch out for. Even labeling your child confidentially to another adult will cause the adult to treat your child differently. For instance, if you mention to your child's teacher that he's your "wild one," the teacher may take special measures to calm him during class—without even giving him the chance to succeed on his own, and whether he's actually "wild" in school or not.

Another mistake is to make use of a "go-to" kid. This is the child you can count on to complete a task competently and without much complaining—so whenever you *really* need something important done, you approach her instead of your other kids. However, anytime you don't share responsibility evenly in an age-appropriate way, you effectively tell your other kids that they're not as significant or capable as your go-to kid. In doing so, you foster an atmosphere of competition. Along these same lines, as your kids get older and you're more comfortable leaving them alone for short periods, it's wise not to put one child in charge of another—this only fuels rivalry and one-upmanship. Instead, each should be responsible for himself and specific tasks—Evan for making lunch and pouring milk, and Jason for cleaning up after the meal.

Putting an end to the use of labels in your household, and accepting each child's ups and downs as they come, will go a long way in reducing the competition between your kids. Remember, they should never be pitted against each other to gain any kind of favor in your eyes, and labels can cause a lifetime of damage in sibling relationships.

In addition to resisting labels, you can use several of the tools you've already learned to make sure each child develops a strong sense of belonging and significance, and to assure them they don't need to compete with their siblings to achieve these.

Mind, Body & Soul Time is invaluable in giving each of your children a healthy dose of your undivided attention twice a day for which they do not have to compete with one another.

If you have one child who seems to pester or demand attention from a sibling, you can even schedule sibling Mind, Body & Soul Time for the pair. This is similar to Mind, Body & Soul Time that you do with your kids, but it's between siblings, so that they spend quality one-on-one time together. They'll develop their relationship and also be able to connect in a positive way rather than through constant negative behavior toward each other. For example, it's obvious why big brother Noah is little Isabelle's hero—he's funny, kind and creative. However, 8-year-old Noah may not always appreciate 4-year-old Isabelle's blatant adoration, and especially when he really just wants to play football with his friends (rather than perform that hilarious voice with her stuffed doggy). By setting aside some time for the two of them to play with each other on a regular basis, Isabelle will know that she'll get her brother's attention, and she doesn't have to whine and pester for it. Accordingly, Noah won't have to feel guilty when he goes off to do his own thing—he knows he'll have plenty of time to play with Isabelle (whom he clearly adores, too) during their Mind, Body & Soul Time together.

Using Encouragement liberally will help ensure that your kids know they're all valuable members of the family, so there will be less competition over their place within the unit. And Training will give each of your children the chance to make meaningful contributions and develop a sense of independence.

So, what if you've eliminated the use of labels, and are successfully using positive tools to give each of your kids a strong sense of belonging and significance, and they're still fighting?

Well, for one, it just means that they're siblings. There's almost nothing you can do to make sure your kids live in perfect harmony all the time. The rest of this chapter will focus on strategies to help your children avoid arguments with each other and work out conflicts between themselves when they happen.

Parent Guidelines for Kids' Fights

Fast-forward a few years, and Maria is now a self-assured second-grader, while Jack is a happy-go-lucky 4-year-old. Like any siblings, the kids maintain a love-hate relationship. First, they're arguing over whose original intent it was to play with the toy toaster and erupting in tears in the back-and-forth battle, and ten minutes later, they're both happily constructing a pretend pet shop with giant building blocks and vowing to go into business together when they grow up.

As with anything, though, the pet shop plan runs afoul when Jack insists they'll be stocking dinosaurs and Maria informs him that's stupid and impossible. At which point Jack retorts that Maria's an ugly booger-faced silly-billy, snatching a purple cat out of her arms and tossing it behind the couch. Unfortunately, one of Jack's toy triceratops gets caught up in the argument, which culminates in his head being pulled off in Maria's effort to "prove," once and for all, that dinosaurs really are completely extinct.

Both children run frantically to Mom, confident that their own particular version of the story will have her gushing over them and banning their sibling to the back porch for a few hours, like the family dog when he's in trouble.

"Mom, Jack says dinosaurs could be for sale in a pet store. Isn't he stupid? And *then* he threw Penelope behind the couch!"

"Mommy, Maria broke my triceratops!" (Delivered with a wail.)

Mommy knows she has her work cut out for her, having fielded such arguments before.

"Why don't you slow down and tell me exactly what happened?" she sighs.

This unleashes a fountain of "he said, she said" and Mom manages to cobble together some version of the story. She deduces that Maria went overboard, as usual. She's concerned that Maria's becoming too bossy and controlling, and isn't understanding enough of her little brother's limitations.

"Maria, you should've known better than to break Jack's triceratops," she says. "Shame on you. You're bigger and stronger than him, but that doesn't mean you should treat him that way. Go to your room."

As Maria stomps off, she hears her mom coddling Jack: "It's okay, honey, we'll fix your triceratops!"

Jack is then allowed to go back to the pet shop and stock whatever animals he chooses. Maria's only consolation is that Penelope the cat is still behind the couch—and out of Jack's reach.

A QUICK POLL of every parent in your neighborhood would likely show that Maria and Jack's situation is pretty typical. Kids argue, the disagreement turns into a full-blown fight and it's solved only when Mommy or Daddy jumps in to play judge and jury, doling out discipline or punishment as they see fit based on the version of the truth that seems most likely. And then a few hours later, it happens again.

To find a long-term solution for handling our kids' fights, though, we first need to really understand them. Going back again to Adlerian psychology, we see that to find the *reason* for the fighting, we need to look to the *result* of the fighting. In most cases, the result is that a parent gets involved, names an "aggressor" and a "victim," and solves the problem.

The payoff for fighting, then, is a big helping of attention for each child who participates—it's a case of an unconscious pursuit of Undue Attention. As in Maria and Jack's case, the "victim" is soothed with hugs or kind words, while the "aggressor" is confirmed as being more powerful than the "victim." We almost encourage a victim mentality, teaching our kids how to show themselves at a disadvantage to gain our favor—leading to a negative sense of belonging. And in the case of the aggressor, we reinforce the idea that bullying can be used to gain a sense of significance through power, albeit negative. So, each child is labeled and each child gets something out of that label. That's quite a payoff! No wonder our kids fight!

But the pitfalls of playing judge and jury go beyond a payoff. When we solve our kids' disagreements for them, we take away a valuable opportunity for them to learn how to work things out between themselves. Lessons in communication, problem solving and conflict resolution go by the wayside whenever we "help."

Of course, it's hard not to intervene. No parent likes to listen to kids berate each other—it's hard on the heart as well as the ears. And we want to keep things fair for our children. We have an inner need to make sure the child we've deemed to be the "aggressor" doesn't get away with his bad behavior, and that the child who seems to be the "victim" has his hurt feelings alleviated. This is all understandable—but remember that you can only control your children's world so much. They won't live in the bubble of their own home for long, and we certainly hope they won't be calling you to dive in and save them from the mean coworker at their first job.

It'll take some work, but there are better ways to handle your kids' fights—and you can help them learn while reducing the amount of fighting you'll have to listen to in the future. The formula goes like this:

1. Ignore now.
2. Train later.
3. Utilize only helpful adult interaction.
4. Put everyone in the same boat.

The next four tools will address each of these steps, and give you some powerful strategies for making your home a more peaceful one.

Stay Out of Fights

The Tool Explained

One of the main payoffs our kids experience when we get involved in their fights is attention. Some children may begin a fight simply to get your attention (after all, they've received your attention in the past whenever they've had a squabble), or they may continue a fight knowing you'll get involved. Just like when a toddler sweetly demands a kiss for every boo-boo, our older kids want to be justified or soothed for the troubles they face—and never more so than when they're in a fierce competition of strength or wits against a sibling.

Removing the attention payoff is simple: Just ignore the fight (or appear to). As with a Consequence, you'll need to reveal your intent in advance. At a calm moment, sit down with your kids and tell them, "I've noticed that when you fight, I often jump in and get involved. But I have confidence that you can find a way to work things out on your own in the future. From now on, I'll be staying out of your fights and leaving it up to you to resolve them."

When a fight erupts, quietly leave the room (or don't enter it if you're not already present). This nonverbal cue will reinforce the fact that they're on their own to figure things out.

And although you should appear to be completely ignoring the fight, you're actually listening discreetly from a distance. This will give you a chance to tune in and determine if your involvement is necessary, as well as what the key issues are and what training you may need to focus on. Most of the time, you won't need to step in.

Virtually all parents find that staying out of fights is quite liberating—it's wonderful not needing to get involved. What's more, within two to three days most parents notice that the number and intensity of fights decrease, since the payoff of attention has been removed.

When to Use It

- Only after revealing it in advance
- Every time your kids argue or fight (unless there's a threat of immediate physical harm)

Why It Works

Staying out of your kids' fights may seem like a simplistic strategy, but there are three key reasons why it works to reduce the number and duration of fights.

First, as we've discussed, it removes a big payoff. When you refuse to get involved, your kids will be more motivated to figure things out and get on with their lives, rather than escalate the fight so Mommy or Daddy will come running to their rescue. If they know they're not going to get your attention, they won't seek it out.

Second, it gives you a chance to take a deep breath and determine whether you really need to jump in. In most cases, you shouldn't have to. However, if you find that your involvement is needed, this pause as you ignore the fight will help you gauge the situation and get ready to implement the strategies you need (found in the next few tools) to facilitate a resolution, rather than play judge and jury yourself.

Third, and most important, by staying out of fights you'll empower your kids to figure things out on their own. You tell them, subconsciously, that you have faith they can handle their own problems and find a workable solution between themselves. And many times, they will. The lessons they'll learn by implementing positive communication, suggesting alternatives and reaching a compromise (or standing their ground at times for something they really believe in) will serve them well in school and throughout their adult lives.

Tips for Success

- Make sure your kids know you're not emotionally invested in their fight in any way. If you can't leave the room (if you're in the car or the grocery store, for instance), try to involve yourself in another activity—turn up the radio or put your focus elsewhere.

- Use this tool in conjunction with the other tools in this chapter for the best results—but always use it consistently, every time your kids fight.

Handling Sibling Road Rage

Staying out of fights can be tough when they're happening directly behind you. The best strategy for handling your kids' car conflicts is to first reveal in advance that "it's not safe for me to drive when you guys are fighting. In the future, if you fight in the car I'm going to pull over and wait until you're finished. When I hear quiet, then we'll continue." Ask your kids to repeat that back to you.

When the next fight happens, don't say a word. Simply pull

over to the side and wait with a good book that you've stashed in your glove compartment. Reading will keep you busy and allow you to appear unfazed, no matter how late you're running to the choir concert.

You can also help quell backseat brawls by controlling the environment. If possible, avoid having siblings who typically squabble sit next to each other. Also, encourage kids to bring things to keep them busy, such as books, iPods or action figures.

TOOLBOX SOLUTION #19

Teach Conflict Resolution Options

The Tool Explained

Ignoring your children's fights is one key part of reducing this behavior long term. But you also need to make sure you give your kids the training they need to work things out on their own—otherwise, they may never learn the positive options for conflict resolution that will help them down the road. It's no longer your job to solve their problems, but it is your job to help them learn how.

This tool is all about training, and practice. It's not easy even for adults to keep their heads in an explosive situation, and it won't be easy for your kids. Just as it's tough for us if someone eats our lunch out of the shared fridge at work, it's difficult for our kids when their toys get taken or broken by a sibling—and we don't always react in a way that makes us proud. But kids *can* learn (as can adults) positive ways for keeping the peace, by role-playing some of the concepts and tools we've already covered in this book. As the resident expert, you'll need to lead the way. Find a calm, teachable time to train your kids, and begin covering, and practicing, the following concepts.

EMPOWERMENT PARADIGM

First, go over the Empowerment Paradigm concepts. Keep it simple, but make sure they understand that they can't control another person (Can you really keep your sister from taking your hair ties? Or make your brother stop poking you in the car?), but they *can* control their environment and themselves.

CONTROL THE ENVIRONMENT

To help your kids control their environment, you'll need to introduce the concept of a private space, if you haven't already done so. Privacy is a right under Adlerian principles—and it's also a useful component of helping your children maintain a sense of order. Kids need to have someplace where they can play and not be interrupted, and also a place to put their treasures where their siblings (or even the family dog) won't be allowed access. Think about it: Would you want your kid brother using your toy makeup as war paint for his battling tribe of aliens? And if you felt like retreating to write in a journal or draw a picture, would you want a sibling critiquing your work the whole time? Even if your kids share a room, they need to know that they can remove themselves or their possessions to a designated area where they won't be disturbed. You can use special bins or organization systems and props such as a bed canopy or a play tent to further distinguish private space, especially in a shared bedroom. You can also schedule private time every day when one child has sole use of the room.

Once private space is established, also designate common areas—which will probably include the living room, a family room and the backyard. Then, implement three house rules to help your kids protect (or share) their personal property:

1. When I choose to play in a common area, I am choosing to invite my siblings to play with me. If I want to play alone, I can play in my room or private space.
2. When I choose to leave my things in a common area, I am sharing them with my siblings. If I don't want my siblings to play with them, I need to keep them in my room or private space.
3. Play fighting is allowed only by mutual consent. In the case of this rule, you'll need to develop some family-recognized word or phrases that everyone must respect, such as "Stop now," to put an immediate end to the roughhousing when one child is done (or getting hurt). Role-play this several times with each child.

Controlling their environment will help your kids avoid conflict in the first place. Additionally, they'll learn how to set and respect boundaries, skills that will serve them well as they grow older and get into situations where the stakes are higher.

DECIDE WHAT *YOU* WILL DO

You'll also need to help your kids learn how to control themselves (since they can't control their siblings) with more strategies for avoiding fights, and empowering them to handle disagreements if they do happen.

First, emphasize to your kids that no one needs to be a victim in a fight—each participant has the choice to stay and fight, or simply ignore and walk away, putting an end to the fight then and there. At the same time, no one needs to be an aggressor. Help your kids recognize common kid techniques that cause or escalate a fight, including tattling, name-calling, destroying property, physical violence or anything that hurts another person. Let your kids know that these aren't acceptable ways to solve a problem, but there are strategies they can use that not only will be more successful, but also will avoid or reduce conflict.

OTHER USEFUL TOOLS

Now it's time to teach the tools you've been working on. Have your kids practice using a Calm Voice—and make sure you use yours consistently, too. Teach them how to ignore the inciting behaviors of their siblings, and Withdraw from Conflict rather than always running to tattle. Work on "I Feel" Statements, which will make each sibling more receptive to the other's point of view.

Also train them how to make a respectful request with an open palm instead of a demand. For instance, "May I have my toy back, please? I'm still playing with it," instead of "Give me my toy back right now!" could help defuse a disagreement. The open palm is recognized by kids as a universal "I come in peace" symbol, and really works with children. Role-play each of these concepts, and return to training as needed until your kids have the hang of it. All of these tools will work together to bring down the intensity of the disagreement and help everyone work out a solution. Remember, too, that many adults haven't mastered these techniques, and you may be revisiting them throughout childhood.

Training will take an investment on your part, but not only will these tools help keep the peace in your home, they'll also prepare your kids for life in a difficult world.

When to Use It

- When you have plenty of time and are in a calm situation
- For young kids, in mini-sessions that focus on the various concepts and are repeated often

Why It Works

Training our kids in correct behavior and life skills is one of our most important jobs as parents—and the only way to pass on some of the most important information they can learn. By taking time for deliberate training in managing (and avoiding) conflict, we empower our kids to solve their own problems, which in turn will work to decrease the number of fights we see and our level of involvement in them.

The concept of "I can't control another person" will resonate with your kids as they see it play out. And the tools will give them the practical, empowering strategies they need to live their lives on their own terms even in the middle of a busy household. Overall, they'll learn that they can have some measure of control over situations in which they would normally feel lost. For instance, a 5-year-old could never hope to overpower a 10-year-old, but with the positive tools she'll learn, she can at least balance the scale. For her part, the 10-year-old learns a few strategies for keeping her prized Barbies away from her little sister's safety scissors.

Tips for Success

- Don't try to train in the heat of the moment. Save this tool for a calm period when you have some time to spend.
- Post the three house rules from page 241 in a visible location

while everyone learns them. You can also post words or pictures to help remind your kids how to deal with conflict.

- Role-play and practice as long as it takes.
- Be patient with your kids' progress.
- Encourage improvement.
- Avoid the urge to remind your kids about the techniques as a fight is unfolding. Instead, ignore the fight and train later—it's not your place to intervene unless the conflict gets out of hand (we'll talk about this in the next tool).
- Set a good example by using these techniques with your spouse or other adults. That may include:
  - □ Ignoring
  - □ Withdrawing from Conflict
  - □ Providing private space
  - □ Implementing the three house rules
  - □ Communicating with "I Feel" Statements
  - □ Using open-palm requests instead of demanding

TOOLBOX SOLUTION #20

Helpful Parent Involvement

The Tool Explained

What happens if you've put the previous two tools into action, but the fight is spiraling out of control? Or what if one child is clearly abusing another? It may be time to step in (immediately, in the case of physical harm). Before you do, make sure you've truly given your kids a fair shot to work it out on their own.

As you get involved, you'll need to adopt a different role and mind-set from what you've had in the past. It's not your goal here to distinguish right from wrong—it's more important in this situation that your kids can use skills they've learned to solve their problem together. Your job is simply to open channels of communication, facilitating a conversation that can put an end to the conflict.

To get started, you can use a technique called "sportscasting." Just as a sportscaster diplomatically addresses both sides after a game, you'll need to acknowledge the feelings of each of your kids, without making judgments. "Wow, you seem really upset" and "You sound angry about this" are a few phrases you can use that won't put anyone on the defensive.

Then, make sure you give both children a chance to tell their side of the story—even if the situation looks clear to you. However, before they begin, tell them you won't listen to blame or finger-pointing—just the facts. It's less important that you get the full story out of your kids than that they feel like they've been heard. You're not trying to determine who was in the right, just helping them air their grievances in a respectful way. Ask your kids to begin with an "I Feel" Statement, such as "I feel angry because . . ." or "I feel frustrated because . . ." This will help them remember the tool they've learned, and also allow them to practice acknowledging and communicating their feelings.

Once you've heard about the problem from both sides, ask what ideas they have to solve it. Then keep your silence and see what your kids come up with. With any luck, one or the other will figure out a solution both can agree to, and your involvement can end.

Sometimes, however, you'll receive only blank stares or a tearful "I don't know." In this case, you can give a few suggestions. Avoid directly solving the conflict for your kids, but instead say things like

"What would happen if we tried taking turns with the baseball bat?" Or "How about if Drew helped you put the head back on your doll so you could play with it again?" Put several workable solutions out there—but it's your kids' job to reach an agreement between themselves.

If your kids still can't resolve their problem, you'll need to move to the next tool.

When to Use It

- When one child is abusing another
- When a fight between your kids is spiraling out of control

Why It Works

Although your ultimate goal is to be able to let your kids work through all their problems on their own, there are times you'll need to step in. And the less you work to control the situation through Helpful Parent Involvement, the more empowered your kids will be to reach their own agreement.

Part of Helpful Parent Involvement is not taking sides. By remaining neutral, you're helping your kids understand that it takes two people to argue, and that as each contributed to continuing and escalating the fight, neither side is guilt-free.

Facilitating a conversation helps your children practice respectful talking and listening during a conflict—skills they'll use time and time again throughout their lives. With enough practice, and with increasing levels of maturity, they'll learn to field their own disagreements.

And finally, when you allow your kids to come to an agreement on their own (even if they need a few suggestions from you), you're validating their competence in resolving conflict and empowering them to solve the problem completely by themselves next time.

Tips for Success

- The less you talk, the better. As much as possible, sit back and let your kids work through things on their own.
- If you need to offer suggestions, make sure you provide more than one so that your kids can still practice reaching an agreement (rather than just taking orders from you).
- Remain calm to bring down the intensity of the fight.
- The eventual solution should be win-win (or at least not win-lose). Make sure both parties are okay with it.

SPORTSCASTING YOUR KIDS' FIGHTS*

How to step in (the play-by-play):

1. Empathize with each of the children and label their emotions ("You seem angry"; "It looks like you're really worried").
2. Encourage each of the children to tell their version, starting with an "I Feel" Statement.
3. Ask for ideas to solve the problem.
4. Keep your silence.
5. If no one speaks after a minute, suggest a few ideas.

*Adapted from Adele Faber and Elaine Mazlish, *Siblings Without Rivalry* (New York: W. W. Norton and Co., 1987), p. 134.

"I feel . . ." like it's time for a good laugh!

When I first implemented this tool with my own two boys, I got quite the unexpected response. After a squabble, I asked my kids to each tell their side of the story, beginning with an "I Feel" Statement. I anticipated something like "I feel angry because . . ." or "I feel hurt when . . ." Instead, the younger one, Brent, stated emphatically, "I feel . . . that Ryan is an idiot."

This wasn't exactly what I was going for, but it certainly gave us all a good laugh! Clearly we had a little more training to do! It's important to remember that making the best use of all the tools and techniques in this book is a work in progress—for you as well as your kids. But with practice, you and your children can both learn to use "I Feel" Statements to *own* your feelings, rather than placing blame on others as so many of us adults are prone to do.

TOOLBOX SOLUTION #21

All in the Same Boat

The Tool Explained

All in the Same Boat is a tool that can be used to end a conflict by making everyone involved experience the same consequences. If your kids can't agree on a solution to their argument—whether it's an idea you suggest or one they develop on their own—then it should be clear that no one "wins."

With All in the Same Boat, you use an Either-Or to deliver a consequence. It could be something like "Either you find a way to share the toy, or I'll put it away for the rest of the day," or "Either you can agree on a flavor of ice cream, or we won't buy any at the store," or "Either you can both work it out, or you'll both have to play in your rooms for a while."

As a type of Logical Consequence, your Either-Or needs to meet the 5 R's. It should be respectful, related, reasonable, revealed in advance (which you're doing naturally by delivering an Either-Or) and repeated back to you.

Many parents have trouble with this tool—especially if they feel like they know who's at fault. Understandably, our gut reaction is often: "Why should Benjamin suffer when he wasn't doing anything?" My question is, do you *really* know? Sure, maybe you saw Big Brother hit Little Brother over the head with a sand shovel, but what you didn't know is that for the past hour, Little Brother has been immediately smashing all the sand castles that Big Brother has created. Big Brother simply lost his patience—which doesn't mean he acted correctly, but his behavior certainly wasn't random. Siblings have long histories with each other, and if you let them, they'll tell you sob story after sob story to justify their actions. But that's not helpful in learning how to handle conflict, and it only reinforces a "victim" mentality.

What's more, it's not our job to make a judgment. We need instead to send the message that it's not important who started the fight. All that matters is who participates. Everyone has the option to ignore it and walk away.

As you're implementing All in the Same Boat, remember that although this is a powerful way to put a quick end to your kids' fights, it's not advisable to simply skip to this tool without first Ignoring, then Training and then using Helpful Parent Involvement. By Ignoring the fight, you let your kids know that you have confidence in their abilities to find a resolution. When you Take Time for Training, your kids learn positive ways to resolve conflict. And supporting them with Helpful Parent Involvement gives your kids another opportunity to solve their own problems as you facilitate communication. If you skip ahead to All in the Same Boat, your kids will miss out on valuable training opportunities and the chance to practice conflict resolution skills.

When to Use It

- When communication and conflict resolution have hit a brick wall
- When your kids can't agree on a workable solution
- Only after employing the previous three tools

Why It Works

All in the Same Boat is a powerful tool that reduces competitiveness, avoids making moral judgments and removes the payoff that kids previously received from their fighting. By taking away any impetus for fighting, it puts the argument to an immediate end.

Competitiveness is a key driving force behind fights, and never more so than when you intervene. With your undivided attention, stakes are high—and each contributor to the argument will want to prove that they're in the right, thus winning your approval. When you deliver the news that everyone will be facing the same consequence, you remove the spirit of competition, and instead put the focus on cooperation. There will be no "winner" and no "loser"—only two kids who are willing to agree or instead face a consequence.

Avoiding moral judgment may not sound like a good thing—after all, don't we want our kids to know right from wrong? Of course we do, but *a fight between siblings always constitutes misbehavior,* whether it's over who broke the toy, or who can jump the highest, or the fact that one used the other's cell phone to call a friend. No one *has to* participate in a fight, and the correct behavior would've been to ignore it and walk away in the first place or work together to come up with a solution everyone can agree on. What's more, by removing ourselves from the "He said, she said" barrage inherent in any sibling fight, and refusing to pass judgment, we help our kids learn that what happens isn't nearly as important as how you handle it.

Finally, All in the Same Boat swiftly and effectively removes any payoff for fighting. It becomes clear that neither one can "win" this battle unless they decide then and there to cooperate. And in fact, everyone will lose if they continue the argument.

With all motivation and ability to keep fighting removed, your kids have no choice but to carry out the agreement they've reached or face the same consequence. They might not be happy, but they've learned that no one benefits from fighting.

Tips for Success
- Continue to remain calm and indifferent to the two "sides" of the argument.
- Refuse to listen to whining—after delivering the consequence and receiving the answer, just walk away.

Fighting the Good Fight
(or Not Fighting at All)

The strategies in this chapter may be simple, but they're not easy. They'll take work and commitment on your part—not to mention from your kids, as they practice new concepts and skills. But the benefits are great. Children who can successfully manage their own difficult interpersonal situations will be at a huge advantage as they negotiate classes, careers and their own families and friendships later in life.

And don't forget the fact that you'll no longer spend time negotiating your kids' arguments for them—and with time and practice, you may not find yourself hearing them fight much at all.

What's more, by fostering an environment in which each child feels valued—without labels or any additional competition—you're setting your kids up for lasting, loving relationships with each other for a lifetime.

Another tool that will help your family grow together and navigate life under the same roof is a Family Meeting. The next chapter will focus on a key way to maintain a harmonious and dynamic family life.

BRINGING EVERYONE TOGETHER

Every school day except Wednesdays, 12-year-old Charles Frederickson attends basketball practice. He also practices Saturday mornings from nine to twelve, and has games once or twice a week. His trumpet lesson is on Wednesdays. Every few months, he participates in a performance, recital or competition—and he's getting quite good.

Ten-year-old Jayda Frederickson is at the gym for gymnastics class two evenings a week, and sometimes attends extra practice on Sunday afternoons. She's also been helping her aunt, who just had a new baby, around the house for a little extra spending money. And she's in the advanced learning program at her elementary school, which often sends her to the library after school to dig into special projects. She likes to sing, so she volunteers for every choir event at school and church.

Although he's only six, Marcus Frederickson is a very involved first-grader. He loves playing with the neighborhood kids, and after discovering that he has some natural talent for soccer, he joined a traveling league. He has out-of-town matches once a month, and practices on Mondays, Wednesdays and Saturday afternoons. He also takes one kiddy class a semester at the local art center.

For her part, Mom serves on the steering committee for the local elementary school, which Jayda and Marcus attend. She volunteers at a soup kitchen two Saturday evenings a month, and also brings meals to new moms through the family's church. She and her best friends have committed to getting together for dinner one evening a month, and in addition, she stops by to check on her elderly mother every couple of days, bringing her groceries or helping her around the house. Oh, and she works a full-time job.

Dad is a full-time college professor, but with his flexible hours, he's often responsible for the kids' doctor and dentist visits, waiting for deliveries at home and running errands between classes when he can. He leads the Sunday evening cultural studies club for the college where he teaches, and always has papers to grade or lessons to plan. And he's never missed a Red Sox game.

WHEW! Hopefully you're not as tired reading this as I am writing it! Take a look at the family's schedule of commitments above, and see if you can find a time when everyone's together under one roof. Chances are, you can pinpoint only a few hours—and most of them are when the family is sleeping.

While this household might represent a somewhat overachieving American family, their schedule isn't too far off from the realities that many of us face every day. It seems that between parents' jobs, kids' activities, and social and volunteer commitments, the only thing we *don't* do nowadays is spend time together as a family.

We've all heard about the perils and pitfalls of being "too busy," but sometimes we can't—or don't want to—change our lives. For instance, you likely wouldn't tell your 11-year-old she can't play basketball, a game she's loved since she made her first basket at age five, just because you don't want to drive her to all the practices, games and out-of-town tournaments. Or maybe, as a single parent, you don't have much choice in how busy you are as you provide for your household on one income. As much as we'd like things to be calmer and less chaotic at times, unless we make a family decision to end extracurricular activities, we'll probably be maintaining our hectic pace for a while. But whether your family is super-busy or laid-back, it's still vitally important for everyone under your roof to spend quality time together on a regular basis. And by now, you should know the value of fostering deep connections, allowing kids to have input into everyday matters and using good communication to solve problems that come up.

The tool in this chapter will give you a power-packed strategy for incorporating all of these things into your family's hectic life. And even while you maintain your busy schedule, you can create a sense of order around it, and keep everyone grounded in a happy, functional home. The tool is called a Family Meeting, and it incorporates all the concepts and strategies we've talked about so far. Your kids will love it, and so will you.

Basic Family Meeting

The Tool Explained

In simple terms, a Family Meeting is Mind, Body & Soul Time spent together as a family every week. These gatherings are a wonderful way to boost everyone's sense of belonging and significance, forge meaningful connections and make sure the whole family is on the same page with all the important things going on in your lives. A Family Meeting provides a forum for all family members to connect, solve problems and simply have fun together. It's a ritual that will promote lifelong bonding and togetherness, while teaching your kids valuable lessons about communication, cooperation, decision making and respect for others.

And if you're recalling a stiff, boring assembly in a conference room with a whiteboard and your boss droning on, think again. Your Family Meetings will be nothing like this—you'll find that they're actually quite fun! I promise.

Let's explore the 5 W's of the Family Meeting.

WHO SHOULD ATTEND?

Everyone who lives under your roof should plan to be there—including grandparents or a live-in nanny. Even if your family comprises only two people—you and your child—it's still a family, and Family Meetings will still help you connect, discuss important matters and ensure that you take time for fun every week.

WHERE SHOULD WE HOLD IT?

Hold your meeting someplace in your home that's comfortable, but doesn't have a lot of distractions. The living room and kitchen table are both great places, but not over dinner if at all possible—the constant clattering of silverware and the "Can you pass the corn?" requests would be too distracting for a Family Meeting.

WHEN SHOULD WE HOLD IT?

Commit to holding a Family Meeting every week. Strive for a regular day and time (Sunday evenings work well for many families), but if you can't, then coordinate a time when everyone will be available. Family Meetings don't need to be long in duration—they can be as short as twenty minutes or as long as an hour.

When your kids know that you plan to meet regularly, they'll come to expect it, and enjoy the time together. What's more, there won't be the sense of "Oh no, *now* we're in trouble!" that you might get if you met only when something was wrong. A weekly commitment can ensure that Family Meetings become a positive time for everyone. And putting them into your regular schedule will make you less likely to miss one.

WHY ARE WE DOING THIS?

Before you begin implementing Family Meetings, you'll need to explain to your kids why they're important. Say, "As a family, we really value everyone's input into family decisions and about problems that may come up. We want to hear what you think! We'll make these fun, so we can all have a good time together every week."

WHAT SHOULD WE TALK ABOUT?

Each Family Meeting will have an agenda, to make sure you cover the important things (including the fun!) and stay on track. As you're beginning to hold Family Meetings, stick to the basics. Your goal is to keep the meeting short and sweet, to ensure success. In the next tool we'll cover more agenda items that you can add when you feel more confident. The basics include the following elements:

Compliments and Appreciations

Open each meeting by going around the table (or living room) and asking each family member to share one positive thing about each of the other family members. It's helpful if a parent can begin, to get the ball rolling and break the ice. For the Frederickson family in the example at the beginning of this chapter, Compliments and Appreciations might sound like this:

Mom Frederickson:

"I really appreciate the way Dad helped out with carpool this week. I was swamped with work and I couldn't have managed everything without him."

"Jayda, I've noticed you've really been putting in a lot of effort on your big book report this week. Keep up the good work!"

"Marcus, thank you for the lovely flowers you planted in my window box. They're so beautiful and I love to look at them!"

"Charles, you were a great friend this week to James for walking his dog while his ankle was healing from its sprain. I'm sure he really appreciates having a neighbor like you!"

Jayda Frederickson:

"Charles, thank you for helping me with my math homework. I understand it a lot better now."

"Mom, I really had fun shopping with you on Saturday!"

"Dad, thank you for fixing my bike."

"Marcus, you always make me laugh! I'm glad you're my little brother."

And so forth.

Compliments and Appreciations might be tough for your kids to come up with at first, but with practice everyone can think of something nice to say. They also may feel awkward giving and receiving compliments—which makes this a great way to Take Time for Training in handling compliments gracefully. But with time, your kids will wait eagerly to hear what their siblings, especially, have to say about them. Soon, this first agenda item will be something that all of your family members look forward to, and it'll set a positive tone for the rest of the meeting.

Calendar

Each Family Meeting is a great opportunity to review everything going on in family members' lives during the week, and for kids to be able to see what's coming up. Set up a master calendar, whether it's a magnetic chart, a day planner or a large wall calendar, and record everyone's events and needs. For instance, mark carpool days, sports events, dates when big homework projects are due, nights when the babysitter will be coming, travel times, volunteer commitments, birthdays and social events. Use stickers to help younger kids tune in—for instance, a soccer ball would denote a practice, or a birthday hat could mark a friend's birthday party. Put the calendar where everyone can see it, but bring it out for a closer look during the Family Meeting. Additionally, you can suggest children eight years and older keep their own calendar—this will help them learn skills such as advance planning, problem solving, decision making and communication.

Reviewing the calendar together will help you manage the chaos in your household and reduce anxiety for everyone. For instance, you can find out before it's too late that your son and daughter need to be on opposite sides of town for different events at the same time while your spouse is out of town. Let your kids help solve the problem; for instance, you can ask, "What can we do to make sure both of you are able to attend your events?" One might suggest carpooling with a friend, or another might be willing to arrive extra early for her event. This will avoid a potential battle, and give your kids practice in working out solutions together.

Allowance

Family Meetings are a great place to hand out your children's allowances. They'll feel extra important if you put each amount into an envelope. The allowance not only boosts a child's significance, but it can be a good motivator for your kids to attend the meeting. If you need to, you can set it up as a When-Then: "When you come to the Family Meeting, then you'll get your allowance for the week."

Snack

Wonderful connections are made over food—and Family Meetings should be no exception. Snacks, whether healthy or indulgent, provide a great bonding opportunity and should be included each time you meet. Just be sure to save them for the end (to maintain a sense of order) and to keep them fun.

Family Fun

Family fun is so important, I always include it as part of the agenda—and you should, too. Not only will you forge positive connections as a family, but you'll be committed to Mind, Body & Soul Time together on a weekly basis. The benefits of having fun as a group, in the Child Ego State, will serve you throughout your lives.

Family fun can be as simple as going around the table and asking each family member to tell a joke, or as involved as heading out on a bike ride together. You could also play a board game, watch a home movie, read a story, play basketball in the driveway and so much more. Be creative, let your kids decide what to do and make sure that everyone can participate. This will end your Family Meeting on a positive note, and have everyone looking forward to the next one.

As you conduct your Family Meeting, be sure to keep the mood light and focus on making it a good experience for everyone. And once you all feel confident with a Basic Family Meeting, you'll know it's time to add a few more agenda items, which you'll find in the next tool.

QUICK-START GUIDE TO FAMILY MEETINGS

1. Pick a weekly time to meet with everyone in your family. Let your family know that you'll be starting to hold Family Meetings because you want to connect and get their input into family matters on a regular basis.
2. Gather everyone in a place with few distractions.
3. Open with Compliments and Appreciations. Then review the calendar. Next, pass out allowance. Serve a snack.
4. And finally, have some Fun!

When to Use It

Weekly, either at regularly scheduled times or when everyone is available

Why It Works

Family Meetings combine all of the tools in this book into one power-packed Mind, Body & Soul Time for the entire family. As you use strategies from Training, Encouragement, "I Feel" Statements and more, this tool will boost your kids' feelings of belonging and significance, as well as solve real-life challenges and provide practical training for the future. With each Family Meeting, your kids will get lots of practice in good communication, problem solving and planning. They'll get a huge dose of positive power as they contribute their opinions and ideas to making important decisions.

And weekly meetings create a fun, positive, useful ritual for your kids to anticipate and look forward to every week. Nowadays, most of our rituals revolve around holidays and other celebrations— with few that occur more than once a year or once every couple of months (unlike the Saturdays at the movies, or Sunday dinners at Grandma's house of yesteryear). Structure and predictability are good for kids of every age, especially when they know that once a week they'll have a set time to connect with the entire family.

Tips for Success

- Solicit your kids' opinions for snacks and family fun. The more involved they are, the more meaningful your Family Meeting will be.
- There's no need to drag out the Family Meeting—if you have extra time, use it for fun. Keep the mood light so that kids look forward to this time every week.
- Make sure your focus is on providing Mind, Body & Soul Time as a family. Connecting and bonding is more important than making sure the calendar is completely up to date.

TOOLBOX SOLUTION #23

Family Meeting—Beyond the Basics

The Tool Explained

Once you've mastered the basics of a Family Meeting and are ready to put this useful tool to even more good use, you can add items to your agenda, as well as the Ground Rules that go along with them. In addition, you'll need to start assigning everyone a role to play in the meeting.

Additional agenda items may include the following:

GENERAL TOPICS

Any family member can bring up anything they'd like to discuss as a family. This could be an upcoming family vacation, birthday party plans, future houseguests and the like.

You might ask your kids which activities they'd like to do on vacation (assuming you've already chosen the destination), or what's most important to them in celebrating an upcoming holiday. Your 8-year-old might bring up the fact that he really wants a family pet, and you can all discuss the merits—and challenges—of bringing an animal into your home.

Keep in mind that even in a democratic family, not everything is up for discussion or debate. It's up to you to determine which issues are non-negotiable, and then stick to them. Matters of health and safety are certainly non-negotiable, as is anything that's not appropriate for kids to weigh in on. For example, you may be faced with a move to another state for your job. It's not up to your kids whether or not to move, but you can ask for their input on how the move will take place, what can be done to make it easier on everyone or what features to look for in a new house. As the parent, you'll need to decide in advance which topics are appropriate to bring to the Family Meeting for discussion. If a topic is a non-negotiable, it might be easier on everyone if you just don't bring it up.

Most important, discussion of General Topics can be a fun time for your family to talk about nonproblematic topics and make decisions that are within everyone's boundaries.

PROBLEM SOLVING

Is the bathroom getting "hogged" every morning? Was there a sibling conflict during the week that didn't get resolved? Is there a trend of family contributions not getting completed? This is the time to discuss—and find a resolution for—any problem that's currently plaguing your family. Any family member can bring it up, and anyone can offer input.

Problem Solving can be a volatile time during a Family Meeting if you're not careful, so I suggest you follow these guidelines:

- Let everyone know that they're expected to use their Calm Voice and use "I Feel" Statements, instead of becoming angry and accusatory.
- Make sure everyone has a chance to contribute, and only one person talks at a time. You can use a "talking stick" or a beanbag to denote the family member who has the floor. If you need to, you can also implement the rule that no one can make a second point until everyone's had a chance to talk.
- Stay on topic. Later, we'll talk about assigning roles to each family member—one role can be the Taskmaster, who will help make sure the conversation stays on track.

Problem Solving is an extremely valuable training tool within a Family Meeting. Your kids will master all kinds of skills, including using appropriate communication, empathy for another's point of view, creative thinking, negotiating, teamwork and reaching consensus. So although it may take a while for everyone to get used to discussing problems in an orderly fashion, it's well worth the effort.

Although you'll probably need to help facilitate discussion of problems at times, your goal should be to let your kids come up with a solution together. They'll feel so much more empowered than if you just "lay down the law," and will gain so much more from the experience. Remember, part of the purpose of a Family Meeting is to get your kids' input as part of your democratic household—you still have the final say when it comes to the non-negotiables, but they'll learn a lot and enjoy a huge boost of significance when they can be a part of the process. Make sure all the adults in your household are on board with this plan, so that your children really do have the floor most of the time.

As an example, maybe some of your kids' shared outdoor toys have been getting broken lately. Instead of allowing your children to place blame, you can facilitate a discussion about how to keep toys in better shape. Listen to your kids' suggestions before offering any of your own. Make sure the decision is one that all can agree with (it's not acceptable for older kids to simply ban the rambunctious 4-year-old from playing with the toys), and then close the conversation until the next meeting to give the plan a fair shot. And avoid deciding based on a majority vote, as this only divides the family into winners and losers. By reaching *consensus*—a decision everyone can live with—you'll promote the use of win-win solutions, negotiation and empathy for others.

Finally, in the interest of teaching, it might be to everyone's benefit if you allow a solution that might not be what you consider the best one. If your kids have decided that to limit bathroom hogging, they're going to implement an open-door policy for brushing teeth and doing hair (after everyone's dressed, of course), refrain from suggesting using a timer instead. You might have to listen to a few fights over sink space, but eventually your kids will either make their idea work or try something new.

Not only will letting your kids help solve family problems teach them important lessons, it will be much more empowering for them than simply being told what to do by Mom and Dad. What's more, when your children participate in coming up with a solution, they'll be much more likely to implement it.

TRAINING

Family Meetings can be the perfect time to Take Time for Training in concepts that pertain to the whole family. For instance, table manners, fire safety and telephone etiquette can all be taught at a Family Meeting through role-play and practice. You can also teach tools you've learned in this book, such as "I Feel" Statements, Withdrawing from Conflict and Calm Voice. Keep the training short and simple—if you need to do more in-depth training, save it for another time.

WHAT CONSTITUTES CONSENSUS?

Consensus is not a majority vote, and it may not be everyone's favorite choice—but it represents a solution that everyone decides is workable. In your Family Meeting, reaching consensus should mean coming to an agreement together.

MEETING ROLES

Your Family Meetings should also assign everyone a role—one for each person under your roof. The roles should change for each meeting, so that everyone gets a chance to be the Meeting Leader, Note Taker, Snack Server, Family Fun Planner, Taskmaster, Calendar Keeper, Problem-Solving Facilitator or any other jobs you decide to use. Even an 18-month-old can be the Napkin Distributor for your snack. And wouldn't it be wonderfully empowering for your 4-year-old to conduct the entire meeting as Meeting Leader? Allowing everyone to play a role will keep everyone involved, let everyone take part in the meeting's success and keep it fun for the whole family, too.

GROUND RULES

Every Family Meeting needs to adhere to some Ground Rules, to keep it running efficiently and to make sure everyone is involved in a positive way. I recommend you stick to the following:

1. *Commit to meeting weekly.* Treat Family Meetings as Mind, Body & Soul Time for the entire family.
2. *Don't bring a problem unless you come prepared with at least one or two possible solutions.* This will help protect your meeting from self-serving rants and gripes that are more about airing grievances than finding a resolution. To nip griping in the bud, say, "Why don't you offer up a few suggestions for solving this problem, and then we'll see what ideas everyone else has."
3. *Decisions require consensus.* We want to cooperate and work together to find a solution that everyone can get behind, or at

least live with. Decisions should work for the good of the family, whether or not each agreement you come to is everyone's top choice. This is different from a majority vote—we don't want to foster an atmosphere of winners versus losers within our families.

4. *Live with decisions for one week.* Once a decision is made, it's important to provide ample opportunity for it to work—or not. You'll soon discover whether the decision was a good one, or if it'll need tweaking at the next Family Meeting. This trial time serves as a Natural Consequence to help your kids learn from their decisions and actions. In fact, in the spirit of training your kids, there may be times when you'll want to go along with a decision even if you know it's not a good one. What's more, it'll promote a united family atmosphere—what you decide as a family, you commit to as a family. This policy will help everyone work as a team.

5. *Everyone has a job.* By asking everyone to play a role (Meeting Leader, Snack Maker, Note Taker, etc.), you can bring everyone into the success of each meeting. Rotate jobs weekly so everyone participates in each role.

6. *Remember the fun!* Always end with an enjoyable family activity—even if it's short. And keep the meeting fun throughout, so your kids will look forward to it each week.

7. *Family Meetings are for all families.* No matter your family's size or configuration, a Family Meeting should be part of your weekly schedule. Every family has calendars, problems and other topics to talk about—and a huge need to have fun together on a regular basis!

When to Use It

Start using Beyond the Basics techniques for your Family Meeting when you're comfortable with a Basic Family Meeting. This could be by week 2, or after a year of mini-meetings, and it will likely depend on the ages of family members and your family dynamic. You can incorporate the new techniques slowly so that everyone has a chance to catch on.

Why It Works

Going Beyond the Basics with your Family Meeting is a great way to open the family conversation even more. These additional agenda items will further expand your kids' skills and opportunities for making meaningful decisions that can have a real impact on your household.

It is said that "you'll never get buy-in without weigh-in," and by allowing your kids to have input into the family's decisions instead of coming up with rules and regulations behind closed doors, you'll gain their support. And when you give them a forum to discuss family problems, you'll send the message that it's everyone's responsibility to contribute—and that everyone can share in the benefits.

Tips for Success
- Post the weekly agenda on the refrigerator or in a place where everyone can add topics to discuss.

Top 10 Family Meeting Pitfalls

Even the best of plans and intentions can be subject to a wide variety of complications—and the Family Meeting is no exception. Following are the top ten problems that derail Family Meetings, and how to avoid them:

10. *Tackling too much, too soon.* Your first few Family Meetings don't need to rival Monday morning updates at the White House. Keep it simple at first, and add more only when you feel like the whole family is ready. Keep it simple!

9. *Parents take over.* If your kids get the feeling that the Family Meeting is just another way for you to advance your own agenda, it won't be successful. Don't take over the meeting!

8. *Too many agenda items.* Especially with younger kids, two to three agenda items is plenty. Then it's time to move on to family fun.

7. *Straying too far off the agenda.* It's easy to get lost in side conversations in any meeting, but you need to keep your Family Meeting on track. If you need to, assign someone the role of Taskmaster to help ensure all topics are addressed, and that the discussion is progressing instead of getting stalled along the way. Stick to the agenda!

6. *Too much business, not enough fun.* Family Meetings may cover serious topics occasionally, but overall they need to be fun and engaging. If your meetings get bogged down with too much of the "boring" stuff, your kids will stop looking forward to them. Limit the number of agenda items, and keep things moving. Focus more on "fun" than on "business."

5. *One person dominates the discussion.* Most families include some members who are more talkative than others—but that doesn't mean everyone's opinion isn't important. It's good practice for everyone to learn to listen to others, and to speak up when they have something to say. As mentioned before, you may want to pass around a talking stick or a beanbag to designate who has the floor. If you need to, implement a rule against making a second statement until everyone has had the chance to speak. Use a talking stick if you think someone will dominate the discussion.

4. *It turns into a gripe session.* If your kids begin to see Family Meetings as a chance to complain about their siblings, their lives, their desperate need for a new cell phone or anything else, you need to get them back on track. The rule of "Don't bring a problem unless you bring at least one or two solutions" will help. Don't let a meeting turn into a gripe session.

3. *Going too long.* It may be tempting to discuss anything and everything that's come up during the week, but making the meeting too long will only tune out and turn off your kids. Keep it short.

2. *Parents solve all the problems.* Your goal should be to bring your children into the decision-making process. If you find yourself (and/or your spouse) coming up with all the ideas or making all the decisions, work on keeping quiet instead—even if there are a few awkward moments when no one says anything at all. Let the democratic process play out, and strive for cooperation, creative thinking and, in the end, consensus. Let kids come up with the solutions to problems.

1. *Families have meetings only when there's a problem.* Be proactive

about meeting weekly so that kids don't come to dread meetings as something the parents plan when they need to hand out more rules or deliver bad news. If there's not much to discuss, that's okay! It's fine to focus on family fun. Don't wait until there's a problem to have a meeting!

SINCE every family is different, every Family Meeting will be, too. The most important thing is that you have the meetings, that you allow your kids input into your home life and that you put most of the focus on fun. By meeting regularly, you'll build the positive skills and emotional connections that will benefit your whole family far into the future.

11

TAKING THE
TOOLBOX HOME

The Normal family has been through a lot of changes in the
past few days, weeks and months. But they've all been good ones.

For instance, the Normal second-grader, who used to fight
back at anything his parents said, now helps out around the house
and turns off the television when asked. Not always happily, of
course, but without the full-blown battle that used to be common-
place. Two days ago, a spontaneous "Thank you" was heard from
his mouth, and every day since last week he's picked up his toys in
the living room before bedtime (having only twice had his remote-
control alien dinosaur relegated to the back closet for being left on
the floor). He's also learned how to vacuum the floor—even the
corners.

Meanwhile, the Normal preteen has not only "magically" become less forgetful, but she's even been showing more respect for her parents. In fact, the girl has uttered the word *whatever* only once today, and it was used in a normal sentence. She, in turn, has felt more respected—she's no longer nagged about her homework and her room "every little minute of every day" (in her words), and hasn't minded pitching in more around the house as much as she thought she would. In a moment of parental joy, she even asked her mom to go "hang out at the mall with me" last Saturday, and solicited Mom's opinion on a new pair of jeans she bought with the allowance money she's been saving.

And let's not forget the Normal preschooler. Even a phone call to order pizza had been too long for the 4-year-old to endure without interrupting at least once, but on Friday Dad was able to pay a stack of bills with only a polite "The batteries ran out in my fire truck, can I have some new ones?" from the boy. And after receiving the batteries, he promptly went back to his play. Bedtime has been a smoother process every night, and the standard four glasses of water (one of which is "too cold," another of which is "too full" and yet another that "has dust in it") have been whittled down to just one, which is what his parents have designated as reasonable for the bedtime routine.

Of course, the Normal parents themselves have undergone some transformations of their own. They do not raise their voices much anymore, except at sporting events and to call the dog in from the backyard. Mom has been able to lighten up and has quit demanding that all the dishes be sparkling clean even *before* being placed in the dishwasher, and Dad has been able to tighten up, not giving into his kids' whims just because, as he says, "you don't understand—he really, really, *really* wanted the candy!" Both are enjoying family life and are a lot more likely to try to come home early from the office than to make up an excuse to stay late so they don't have to be the one refereeing the typical dinnertime "Eat your green beans and don't throw anything else at your sister" battle.

Everyone's happier, and they all spend time together on a regular basis. Yes, the Normal family still has room to grow, but they've already come a long way.

COULD this be your family? It's my hope that the information, tools and strategies in this book have given you a solid start in creating the fun, harmonious and empowering atmosphere in your house that you've been dreaming of ever since your kids were first able to verbalize the word *"No!"*

The Normal parents have implemented tools like Mind, Body & Soul Time, Calm Voice, Encouragement, Take Time for Training, When-Then Routines, Consequences, Choices, Ignore Undue-Attention Requests and the rest to help shape their family and foster positive changes. Although they will still face challenges, especially as their kids grow and change, they've laid the groundwork by building belonging and significance, improving their communication and refusing to engage in power struggles or endlessly nag their kids.

These tools don't come naturally—in fact, many are the exact opposite of what you'd normally do. They're also not easy, and the information is a lot to absorb. But you've already taken the first step by reading this book, and as you apply the tools, you should begin to see results quite soon. Celebrate each success—you've earned it! Remember that any progress in the right direction is still progress, and it's something you can be proud of for yourself and for your children.

It's okay to take it slow—implement new tools as you feel ready, and give yourself time to practice and adjust to your new parenting skills. Your family may never be perfect, but they can be happier, more successful in their everyday lives and more prepared for adulthood thanks to the strategies you've learned.

Avoiding Backsliding

At times, and especially when you encounter new or particularly challenging misbehaviors with your kids, you may find it tough to keep your temper and calmly deliver an Either-Or (or Withdraw from Conflict, or Invite Cooperation and so on). Or, you may simply forget the tools that you've learned, and be left speechless (or yelling) as your child wheelies the grocery cart down the cereal aisle. I completely understand—we've all been there.

If you find yourself ordering, directing and correcting your kids, raising your voice at them or getting sucked into power struggles, you might be backsliding. If you notice these behaviors in yourself, first be encouraged that you at least know the difference. Then you can begin to apply the tools again (be sure to review them first), working on addressing your own actions and your kids' misbehaviors.

To avoid backsliding in the first place, there are steps you can take to keep the information fresh in your mind, so the next time you need to enlist "I Feel" Statements or to Decide What *You* Will Do, you can do so without hesitation. Pick a few of the following strategies to implement, and you'll find that you'll always have your parenting Toolbox handy.

Strategies for Staying Fresh

- Reread one chapter of this book each week.
- Use sticky notes and other visual reminders to keep the tools you're working on right in front of you.
- Discuss the techniques and information you've learned with your spouse and/or other caregivers.
- Set goals for yourself. Goals could include training each child in one new task or behavior each week, or finding three encouraging things to say to each child every day. When you're comfortable with one goal, pick a new one to challenge yourself with.
- Employ the Start, Stop and Continue technique: Pick three things you'd like to start doing (operating more from the Child Ego State, Inviting Cooperation, etc.); three things you'd like to stop doing (getting involved in your kids' fights, bossing your kids around, etc.); and three things you'd like to continue doing (Mind, Body & Soul Time, Family Meetings, etc., assuming you've already implemented these tools). Reevaluate every week or two.

GOALS

Five goals for five weeks:

Week 1: _____

Week 2: _____

Week 3: _____

Week 4: _____

Week 5: _____

To DOWNLOAD and print copies of this chart and the one on the following page to hang on your refrigerator, visit www.positive parentingsolutions.com/book-resources.

START, STOP, CONTINUE

Three things I'd like to start:

_____

_____

_____

Three things I'd like to stop:

_____

_____

_____

Three things I'd like to continue:

_____

_____

_____

The Toolbox Applied

Chances are, you've faced many of the misbehaviors highlighted in this book, from clinging and acting helpless to ignoring any and all requests for help around the house. And you'll probably see new ones develop as your kids grow and change. Fortunately, the Toolbox is always there for you, and the techniques work whether your child is in diapers or a marching band uniform.

When a misbehavior appears (whether it's repeated or brand-new), make sure you keep in mind that all behaviors are goal-oriented. At the root, your child is seeking a sense of belonging and significance—a child's hard-wired emotional needs. Misbehavior can usually be addressed in a variety of ways depending on the situation, but the better you can tailor your response to your child's mistaken goal (chapter 8), the more success you'll have in correcting the problem long term.

Whether you've discovered a misbehavior you're not sure how to handle, or you simply want to review some strategies, the chart on pages 283–284 will help you find the information you need. I've listed many of the most common misbehaviors (some are grouped because they have similar causes and solutions), as well as tools to use in the moment and tools to help address the misbehavior at its root so that it's less likely to happen again. If you need a more thorough review of specific tools, I'd encourage you to reread the tool in full, and I've listed page numbers to help you do that.

Misbehaviors Demystified

The Fundamental Tools

One thing that all of the misbehaviors listed on the chart have in common is that *each one* needs to be addressed long-term through the following five tools:

- *Mind, Body & Soul Time* (page 35). This fosters a strong sense of belonging and significance for your children.
- *Calm Voice* (page 60). When you speak calmly, you reduce the intensity level and invite cooperation.
- *Encouragement* (page 83). Use encouraging phrases regularly to bolster your child's sense of significance and reinforce positive behavior.
- *Take Time for Training* (page 113). The goal of parenting is to teach your child how to behave in positive ways and equip them through practical knowledge and skills for greater independence.
- *Choices* (page 121). Offering meaningful choices throughout the day gives positive power and the feeling that the child has some control over his life.

Each of these tools will prevent a host of misbehaviors simply by helping your child recognize and gain confidence in the correct behavior. As you address the misbehaviors below, consistently apply each one of the fundamental tools for an overall improvement in behavior, in addition to the specifically recommended tools in the chart. Also, be sure to avoid the Parent Ego State as much as possible, and limit ordering, directing and correcting your children. Keeping these things in mind will help foster a respectful, positive atmosphere in which you can empower your children for future success.

In addition, keep in mind that things like avoiding labels and limiting your ordering, correcting and directing will also go a long way to inspire the kind of good behavior you'd like to see in your kids.

The Misbehavior	In the Moment	Preventive Measures (in addition to the fundamental tools, p. 282)
Back talk, attitude, disrespect, negotiating, badgering, arguing, demanding "No!" "Why do I have to do it?" "Whatever!"	Withdraw from Conflict (p. 205) When-Then (p. 138) Either-Or (p. 167)	Use "I Feel" Statements (p. 207) Decide What You Will Do (p. 130) Make When-Then Routines the Boss (p. 142) Invite Cooperation (p. 202)
Whining, acting helpless, clinging, interrupting "Hold me!" "I can't do it, I need your help."	Ignore Undue-Attention Requests (p. 190) When-Then (p. 138)	Decide What You Will Do (p. 130) Avoid Special Service (sidebar, p. 197) Use Attention Overload (p. 193)
Repeated forgetfulness	Allow Natural Consequences to play out (p. 152)	Make When-Then Routines the Boss (include checklist as part of the routine) (p. 142) Decide What You Will Do (p. 130) Reveal Natural Consequences (p. 155) Avoid Special Service (sidebar, p. 197)
Tantrums	Withdraw from Conflict (as long as child is in a safe place) (p. 205) Stop Talking and Take Action (sidebar, p. 170)	Make When-Then Routines the Boss (p. 142)
Homework battles, music practice	Make When-Then Routines the Boss (p. 142) When-Then (p. 138) Allow Natural Consequences to play out (p. 152)	Offer Choices (p. 121) Control the Environment (p. 133) Reveal Natural Consequences (p. 155) Avoid Special Service (sidebar, p. 197) Make When-Then Routines the Boss (p. 142) Note: Your child may have a learning difference that makes homework more challenging. If you or your child's teacher thinks this is a possibility, consider an assessment and professional resources.

The Misbehavior	In the Moment	Preventive Measures (in addition to the fundamental tools, p. 282)
Aggression (hitting, biting, kicking, etc.)	Control the Environment (remove the child from the situation) (p. 133) Decide What *You* Will Do (p. 130) Implement Logical Consequences (p. 160)	Reveal Logical Consequences (p. 161)
Chore battles, messy room	Use When-Then (p. 138) Implement Logical Consequences (p. 160)	Make When-Then Routines the Boss (p. 142) Reveal Logical Consequences (p. 161) Invite Cooperation (p. 202) Use "I Feel" Statements (p. 207) Decide What *You* Will Do (p. 130) Hold Family Meeting (p. 256)
Sibling fighting, tattling	Stay Out of Fights (p. 236) Use Helpful Parent Involvement (p. 244) Use All in the Same Boat (p. 248)	Teach Conflict Resolution Options (p. 239) Avoid Labels ("victim" and "aggressor") (p. 229) Use "I Feel" Statements (p. 207) Hold Family Meeting (p. 256)
Potty talk, swearing	Decide What *You* Will Do (ignore the behavior and walk away) (p. 130) Withdraw from Conflict (p. 205)	Reveal Logical Consequences (that you choose not to listen and will walk away) (p. 161)
Mealtime battles	Implement Logical Consequences (p. 160)	Offer Choices (p. 121) Take Time for Training (let kids help with meal prep, menu planning) (p. 113) Reveal Logical Consequences (p. 161)
Bedtime, bathtime and morning battles	Offer Choices (p. 121) Use When-Then (p. 138) Make When-Then Routines the Boss (p. 142)	Make When-Then Routines the Boss (p. 142) Invite Cooperation (p. 202)
Potty training struggles	Offer Choices (p. 121) Use When-Then (p. 138)	Take Time for Training (p. 113) Make When-Then Routines the Boss (p. 142)

Your Changing Family

Think back for a minute to your frame of mind when you first picked up this book and started reading. You may have just battled your 8-year-old about the injustice of asking her to bring her laundry into the laundry room, not to mention a million other similar tragedies. It might have taken a candy bar *and* a new toy just to get your 3-year-old through your most recent grocery store visit. Maybe you were regularly running trips to and from your children's school to deliver mittens, sports equipment and lunches. And it's possible that your enjoyment of parenting waned even before your kids were done with sippy cups.

If you've begun to implement the tools you've learned, chances are your family is already starting to turn over a new leaf. While all your household's behavior problems haven't magically disappeared, they've probably begun to dissipate. And what a change! Just like the Normal family, your family is likely happier and more functional already.

I encourage you to keep at it, whether your results so far have been groundbreaking or a bit more subtle. Your kids are on their way to becoming capable, independent, successful adults, and you're having fun again. Congratulations, and my best wishes go with you as you continue to love, train and parent your children through the wonderful adventure of childhood!

Acknowledgments

My sincere thanks to Judith Regan, who during a radio interview posed the question "Really, why haven't you written a book?" I'll always be grateful to you for giving me the nudge I needed and for introducing me to a fabulous agent.

Many thanks to my literary agent, Paul Fedorko, whose long list of well-known clients has never gotten in the way of making me feel like I'm his most important priority. Paul, your patience and tenacity throughout this process were unwavering. Thank you!

Thank you to the lovely and talented Harriet Bell for helping me shape my ideas for this book.

Thank you to Mary Odegaard for your amazing editorial help and for sharing my vision for this book. You are a dream to work with, and I am grateful for your creativity and skill in making my words and ideas so much more interesting than I could on my own.

My thanks to my editor, Sara Carder at Tarcher/Penguin, for understanding firsthand the challenges of motherhood and believing that this book would help parents find a better way to navigate the tricky moments and enjoy parenting a lot more. Thank you for taking this leap with me and for your patience every step of the way.

My sincere thanks to Andrew Yackira at Tarcher/Penguin for being amazingly organized and responsive. Your attention to detail is a rare gift.

To Vivian Brault, founder of Directions, thank you for salvaging my parenting journey and for counseling me to "adopt and adapt." I hear your sweet words of inspiration and encouragement every single day.

My gratitude to Jane Nelsen, Ph.D., for creating the Positive Discipline program and for inspiring so many parents and parent educators worldwide. Because of you, millions of children are growing up with the dignity and respect they deserve.

Thank you to a team of passionate and highly skilled parenting educators—Kim Dillon, Leslie Marshall, M.D., Lisa Brown and Hollis Bruton—who were instrumental in shaping many of the concepts presented in this book. Thank you for sharing the Positive Parenting Solutions program and for changing the lives of so many families.

Thank you to Lisa Earle McLeod for supporting, inspiring and coaching me from the beginning of the project. I have been grateful for your friendship since our early days of sales training!

Thank you to Jill Dykes, my caring, committed and creative

publicist and friend. Everyone needs a "Stan the Caddy" in her life, and you are the best I could ever imagine. Thanks for being as committed to the vision as I am.

To my siblings, Heidi Miller Kelly, Karen Schoener Baldry and John Miller—thank you for putting up with my bossiness all these years and still managing to love and support me. You are amazing people, and you inspire me in so many ways.

My family tree has many branches, and for that I'm blessed. Thank you to all of my loving and supportive parents and in-laws: Gloria and Hans Wildschutte, Al and Pat Schoener, John and Sue Miller, and Gerry and John McCready.

To my oh-so-patient husband, thank you for keeping every ball in the air and giving me the time and space needed to write this book. You are the best partner ever—in parenting, in business and in life. Our kids are so lucky to have you as their dad.

Thank you to my favorite people in the world, Ryan and Brent. I have always wanted you to know that being your mom is the best and most important job I'll ever have. I love the people you are—not just because you're my kids, but because every day with you blesses me with love, joy, humor and faith. Seriously, guys, is there another family that has as much fun as ours? I love you dearly.

Index

About the Author

Parenting expert Amy McCready is the founder of Positive Parenting Solutions, and a champion of positive parenting techniques for happier families and well-behaved kids. Her tools, delivered in person and online worldwide through her training program, have empowered thousands of parents to correct their kids' misbehaviors *without* nagging, reminding or yelling.

Amy's parenting success developed partly from inspiration and partly out of pure necessity. As a mother of two young children, she recognized that she, like most parents she knew, was lacking the skills, knowledge and tools needed to effectively address negative behavior.

Amy took the initiative to study the principles of Adlerian psychology and positive discipline, and began implementing the principles with her own children. The results were immediate and astonishing—and she knew she had to share what she'd learned with other parents. Drawing on her experience in development and delivery of training programs for Fortune 500 companies, Amy created a parenting curriculum, the Breakthrough Course, which was the foundation for Positive Parenting Solutions. She took her class online in 2008, and since then has helped thousands of moms and dads, who rave about their own success and their happier homes. She has based *If I Have to Tell You One More Time* . . . on the course, in hopes that the book will continue this powerful legacy.

A regular parenting contributor to NBC's *Today* show, Amy has also appeared on *Rachael Ray*, MSNBC's *Dr. Nancy, Fox & Friends, Martha Stewart*, CNN, and elsewhere. She received her bachelor of science degree from Penn State University and is a certified Positive Discipline Parent Educator.

Amy has been married to her husband, Dave, for more than twenty years and is the mother of two boys—Ryan and Brent. The family lives in Raleigh, North Carolina.

If you enjoyed this book, visit

www.tarcherbooks.com.

and sign up for Tarcher's e-newsletter to receive special offers, giveaway promotions, and information on hot upcoming releases.

TARCHER
PENGUIN

Great Lives Begin with Great Ideas

New at **www.tarcherbooks.com**
and **www.penguin.com/tarchertalks**:

Tarcher Talks, an online video series featuring interviews with bestselling authors on everything from creativity and prosperity to 2012 and Freemasonry.

If you would like to place a bulk order of this book, call 1-800-847-5515.